KU-496-459

Contents

ESSENTIAL MADRID	4–18
Introducing Madrid	4–5
A Short Stay in Madrid	6–7
Top 25	8–9
Shopping	10–11
Shopping by Theme	12
Madrid by Night	13
Eating Out	14
Restaurants by Cuisine	15
If You Like...	16–18

MADRID BY AREA	19–106
PALACIO AND THE WEST	20–42
Area Map	22–23
Sights	24–37
Walk	38
Shopping	39
Entertainment and Nightlife	40
Restaurants	41–42

CENTRO	43–66
Area Map	44–45
Sights	46–59
Walk	60
Shopping	61–62
Entertainment and Nightlife	63–64
Restaurants	65–66

JERÓNIMOS AND THE EAST	67–80
Area Map	68–69
Sights	70–77
Shopping	78
Entertainment and Nightlife	79
Restaurants	79–80

CHUECA AND THE NORTH	81–94
Area Map	82–83
Sights	84–90
Walk	91
Shopping	92
Entertainment and Nightlife	93
Restaurants	94

FARTHER AFIELD	95–106
Area Map	96–97
Sights	98–102
Excursions	103–106

WHERE TO STAY	107–112
Introduction	108
Budget Hotels	109
Mid-Range Hotels	110–111
Luxury Hotels	112

NEED TO KNOW	113–125
Planning Ahead	114–115
Getting There	116–117
Getting Around	118–119
Essential Facts	120–121
Language	122–123
Timeline	124–125

CONTENTS

Introducing Madrid

In 1561, King Felipe II made Madrid capital of what soon became the world's biggest empire. Today, the grandeur remains: churches and museums, palaces and parks. But there are also medieval lanes and modern skyscrapers. That's why Madrid is unique.

Nowhere else in the world is the past so close to the present. Nuns and monks still live and worship in convents and monasteries that date back for centuries. Shops still make traditional cakes and breads; locals still stop for olives and a small glass of wine in the way that their forebears have done for centuries. But Madrid is also a city known for its exciting modern architecture, for its trendy small hotels, for its nightlife, with bars and clubs open till dawn…and even later at weekends. While thousands flock to watch the traditional rites at the world's most famous bullring, even more fans head for the Estadio Santiago Bernabéu to watch Real Madrid, arguably the most famous football club in the world.

No other city on the planet has three art galleries of such high quality within a few minutes' walk of each other. But Madrid has dozens of smaller museums that are less crowded and give an insight into the glory and grandeur that was imperial Spain. And it is all so walkable. Stroll around or, if your feet complain, take one of the cleanest, safest and cheapest public transport systems in the world. It is easy to get anywhere in minutes.

This is a city where you need to go with the flow. Only a foreigner eats dinner as early as nine at night; only a foreigner walks the boiling pavements on an afternoon in high summer; only a foreigner spends a whole evening at the same tapas bar. So do as locals do: try different tapas at different bars, sit down to dinner at 10pm, take an afternoon nap, then stay up to the small hours.

Facts + Figures

- The population of Madrid is 3.2 million.
- Madrid is Europe's third-largest city, after London and Berlin.
- Madrid is the highest capital in Europe (646m/2,120ft).

SIMPLY THE BEST

FIFA, football's world governing body, recognized Real Madrid as the world's best football club of the 20th century. You can tour their stadium, named for their former president, Santiago Bernabéu. He put up the idea of the Intercontinental Cup, a match between the champions of Europe and the champions of South America.

CAPITAL CITY

Madrid may be the capital of Spain but only by name. It is locked in a perennial rivalry with equally self-important Barcelona for the honour of being cultural and sporting capital of the country. The two cities are constantly striving to outbid each other in the international events they stage and their cutting-edge architecture.

MOVIE MAGIC

Acclaimed Spanish cinema director Pedro Almodóvar has always derived great inspiration from his home city. Many of his films, including the breakthrough *Women on the Verge of a Nervous Breakdown* (1988), nominated for an Oscar, are set in Madrid. *Labyrinth of Passion* (1982) was partly shot in the Rastro street market where Almodóvar once had a stand.

A Short Stay in Madrid

DAY 1

Morning To beat the crowds in the city's three great museums, you need a prompt start. For the **Museo Nacional Reina Sofía** (▷ 47), use the new extension entrance to the museum (off the Glorieta de Carlos V), still undiscovered by the main rush. Go straight up to see Picasso's *Guernica*, then work your way down.

Lunch Once the crowds build up at the museum, take the Metro across to Serrano for a smart lunch at **Sula** (▷ 80) or any of the myriad cafés.

Afternoon Now hit the shops. Work your way up Serrano to the **ABC Serrano Shopping Centre** (▷ 92), a gallery of smart boutiques. Stroll down the streets called Goya, Velázquez and Ortega y Gasset. Then go back to your hotel for a siesta.

Evening Linger over tapas in the bars on and around the Plaza de Santa Ana. As well as traditional haunts, such as the Cervecería Alemana, there are contemporary wine bars, such as the **Vinoteca Barbechera** (▷ 66). Stroll down to the **Museo Thyssen-Bornemisza** (▷ 48) and soak up some culture. In July and August, the museum stays open late during *Noches de verano*, Summer Nights.

Dinner Afterwards, still in the Museo Thyssen-Bornemisza, dine at the **El Mirador del Museo restaurant**, on the terrace, high above the city.

Later The Spanish love to stay up late, late, late. Hit a popular club such as the **Café Central** (▷ 63) for jazz or the **Casa Patas** (▷ 63) for flamenco. And if you are still going strong at 4am, join the locals at **Chocolatería San Ginés** (▷ 65) for hot chocolate before heading for bed.

Morning If it is a Sunday morning, then do what everyone does: go to **El Rastro** (▷ 53). This swirling mix of outdoor markets and shops has everything from cheap toys, pottery and clothing to expensive antiques and leather goods. Make sure that you have no tempting handbag or wallet on view. Afterwards, drift through the narrow lanes towards the **Plaza de Tirso de Molina**, with its cheerful flower stands, smart new paving, fountains and statue of Tirso de Molina himself. The real name of this playwright was Gabriel Tellez, and he is best remembered for his character, Don Juan. Stroll on east through the old city streets and join locals grazing along Calle de Jésus at tapas bars such as **Cervecería Cervantes** (▷ 65).

Lunch Instead of a big meal, continue hopping in and out of the line of tapas bars along the street. Have dessert at **La Esquina del Café** (▷ 65).

Afternoon Cross the Paseo del Prado and watch *madrileños* at play in the **Retiro Park** (▷ 73). There are puppet shows for little children; boats for hire on the lake; live concerts in summer, when most people are happy to stretch out on the lawns and snooze.

Evening Another authentic Madrid experience is the *zarzuela*. Part Gilbert & Sullivan, part Feydeau farce, these are Spanish comic operas. The music is jolly, the plots are silly, so you don't need to understand the language. The **Teatro de la Zarzuela** (▷ 64) also stages ballet and dance.

Dinner To keep the Spanish experience going, dine nearby at **Taberna Maceira** (▷ 66), where crowds pack in elbow-to-elbow at wooden tables for simple, hearty, Galician dishes.

Top 25

▶ ▶ ▶

Casa de Campo ▷ 24
Take a break from the artworks in Madrid's vast 'green lung'.

Catedral de la Almudena ▷ 25 Madrid's most important church has an impressive clifftop setting.

Ermita de San Antonio de la Florida ▷ 26
Superb Goya frescoes in the chapel where he is buried.

Real Madrid ▷ 100
Spain's most illustrious football club has its home at the impressive Santiago Bernabéu stadium.

Real Academia de Bellas Artes ▷ 54–55 The Fine Arts Academy is best known for its Goya self-portraits.

El Rastro ▷ 53 For bargains galore, the legendary Sunday market still attracts locals and visitors alike.

Puerta del Sol ▷ 52 The 'gateway of the sun' has been the heart of the city since the 15th century.

Puerta de Alcalá ▷ 75
The neoclassical gateway to Madrid, one of the great symbols of the city, is dramatically lit at night.

Plaza de Toros ▷ 98
Its sheer scale makes the bullring impressive, even if you don't come to watch a fight.

Plaza de Oriente ▷ 35
Elegant, pedestrianized square that is a welcome haven of peace in the city.

Plaza Mayor ▷ 51
Madrid's handsomest square, famous for its frescoed Casa de la Panedería.

Plaza de la Cibeles ▷ 74 The Cibeles Fountain is the city's best-loved landmark.

These pages are a quick guide to the Top 25, which are described in more detail later. Here they are listed alphabetically, and the tinted background shows which area they are in.

Monasterio de las Descalzas Reales ▷ 50
16th-century convent that is a treasure house of artwork.

Monasterio de la Encarnación ▷ 27
Former convent famous for its reliquaries.

Museo de América ▷ 30 Outstanding museum dedicated to the art and culture of the Americas.

Museo Cerralbo ▷ 28–29 The home and artworks of a 19th-century marquis.

Museo Lázaro Galdiano ▷ 84–85 Eclectic collection of *objets d'art*.

Museo Nacional Reina Sofía ▷ 46–47 Spain's national museum of modern art.

Museo del Prado ▷ 70–71 Madrid's biggest visitor attraction, this incomparable collection contains more than 8,000 paintings.

Museo Sorolla ▷ 86–87 Museum dedicated to the the life and works of 'the Spanish impressionist'.

Museo Thyssen-Bornemisza ▷ 48–49 One of the finest privately amassed art collections.

Museo del Traje ▷ 31 Dress up in 18th-century clothing at Madrid's most exciting new museum.

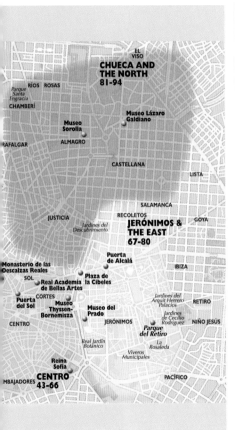

Parque del Retiro ▷ 72–73 Enjoy the shady paths and formal gardens of Madrid's central park.

Parque del Oeste ▷ 34 Madrid's most attractive green space is ideal for a summer stroll.

Palacio Real ▷ 32–33 The vast 18th-century Royal Palace is an outstanding historical monument.

ESSENTIAL MADRID TOP 25

◄ ◄ ◄

9

Shopping

Since the 1980s, out-of-town malls have sprung up and international chains have crept in. But fears that late 20th-century shopping practices would kill off Madrid's many unique little stores have been largely unfounded, and the range of shopping experiences available for visitors is wonderfully diverse. It's these contrasts between the best on the international scene and some superbly idiosyncratic outlets that make Madrid shopping so serendipitous.

A Bit of Everything

It's not just what shops sell that provides a contrast—how they look is also varied. Temples of consumerism in steel and glass happily rub shoulders with cramped, dark shops where the stock is piled high and the merchandise specialized beyond belief. Few other world capitals have as many stores devoted to so many oddities—outsize corsetry, plaster statuary, crystallized violets. This gives Madrid shopping a special appeal, whether you're after easy-to-carry souvenirs or seriously self-indulgent retail therapy, or you simply enjoy window-shopping.

Clothes and Accessories

Madrid has branches of some of Spain and Europe's best-known fashion stores, as well as

---

WHERE TO SHOP

Ask a *madrileño* where to find the city's shopping heart and the answer is bound to be around Calle Preciados, the pedestrianized drag that connects Puerta del Sol with the Gran Vía. Here you'll find branches of all the big chain stores, as well as Madrid's biggest department store, and everything from fashion to food. Smarter by far are the quiet, well-heeled streets of the Salamanca district, home to the big designer names and luxury stores of all description. The best places to trawl for souvenirs are around the Plaza Mayor and the surrounding Los Austrias district, or Malasaña. Head for Chueca for cutting-edge style and street fashion.

Flamenco shop; designer store; flea market; legs of ham (top to bottom)

the latest in the stylish, chain-store fashion, for which Spain is renowned. Spanish leather shoes, bags and belts are some of the best in Europe, and excellent value.

Gifts

For gifts, you'll find goods from all over Spain, ranging from the tasteful fringed and embroidered shawls and *mantillas*, warm winter capes, elegant hats, delicate china, traditional ceramics and damascene work, to the marvellously tacky (plastic flamenco dolls, a poster of a *torero* with your name on it and metal Don Quixotes).

Food

Food makes a great souvenir or gift. In addition to the obvious olive oil, nougat or chocolate, hunt down saffron, wonderful dried nuts, seeds and the fruits so loved by the Spanish. Or look for convent-baked biscuits or cakes, vacuum-packed *jamón* (dry-cured ham), *chorizo* (spicy sausage) or *morcilla* (unctuous black pudding).

Tax Refunds and Sales

IVA (sales tax) is added at seven per cent on food and 16 per cent on most other items. Non-EU visitors can reclaim the IVA on purchases, but the total must be at least €90.15, paid in a single store in a single day. Stores taking part display a Tax-Free shopping sticker. For more detailed information, see www.okspain.org. Sales generally run from mid-January to February, and July to August.

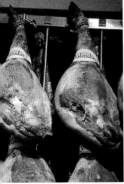

Flea market; lace fans; shop window (top to bottom)

MARKETS

Markets are not only a window into everyday life, but also the perfect place to pick up a picnic to eat in the park. Some of the best are La Cebada (🚇 La Latina)–for a huge range of goods and low prices; El Rastro (🚇 La Latina)–the famous Sunday market; and La Paz (🚇 Serrano)–quality and varied produce aimed at the prosperous Salamanca inhabitants.

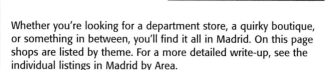

Shopping by Theme

Whether you're looking for a department store, a quirky boutique, or something in between, you'll find it all in Madrid. On this page shops are listed by theme. For a more detailed write-up, see the individual listings in Madrid by Area.

ALL UNDER ONE ROOF

ABC Serrano Shopping Centre (▷ 92)
Centro Comercial Príncipe Pío (▷ 39)
El Corte Inglés (▷ 61)
FNAC (▷ 62)
El Jardín del Serrano (▷ 78)
Mercado de Fuencarral (▷ 92)
VIPS (▷ 62)

ANTIQUES AND GIFTS

Felix Antigüedades (▷ 61)
Galería de Arte Victoria Hidalgo (▷ 78)
Galerías Piquér (▷ 62)
Museo del Prado (▷ 78)
Museo del Traje (▷ 39)
Stamps and Coins Market (▷ 62)

FASHION/ ACCESSORIES

Fabendi (▷ 78)
Massimo Dutti Woman (▷ 39)
Pull & Bear (▷ 39)
Purificación García (▷ 92)
Trucco (▷ 39)
Zara (▷ 62)

FOOD AND WINE

Antigua Pastelería del Pozo (▷ 61)
Cacao Sampaka (▷ 92)
Mariano Madrueño (▷ 62)
Reserva y Cata (▷ 92)
La Violeta (▷ 62)

SHOES/ ACCESSORIES

Ioli (▷ 92)
Lurueña (▷ 39)
Tino González (▷ 39)

SOMETHING DIFFERENT

Berbería del Sahara y El Sahel (▷ 39)
Coronel Tapiocca (▷ 78)
El Flamenco Vive (▷ 61)
Homeless (▷ 92)
Imaginarium (▷ 78)
Natura Selection (▷ 78)
Perfumería Alvarez Gomez (▷ 78)
Piel de Toro (▷ 78)
Toni Martin (▷ 39)

TRADITIONAL

Amparo Mercería (▷ 61)
Antigua Casa Talavera (▷ 61)
Casa de Diego (▷ 61)
Casa Jiménez (▷ 61)
La Favorita (▷ 61)
Guitarras Javier (▷ 92)
Guitarras Ramírez (▷ 62)
Seseña (▷ 62)

Madrid by Night

Madrid has a year-round agenda of cultural evening events, from opera, orchestral concerts, plays, dance and original-language films to jazz, flamenco and Latin American music. Get information in the weekly entertainment guide *Guía del Ocio* and reserve tickets for concerts and plays via www.entradas.com (tel 90 222 16 22) or Localidades Galicia (tel 91 531 27 32; www.eol.es/lgalicia) ticket lines.

A Quiet Evening

With little hope of a restaurant dinner before 9, you might want to take your evening stroll before you eat. Touristy though it is, the Plaza Mayor looks great by night; from here you can wander through buzzing Huertas down to the wide Paseo del Prado, a wonderful place in summer for a stroll and a drink at a *terraza*. A few minutes' walk away lies the Retiro Park, perfect on balmy evenings. For window shopping, head for the elegant streets of Salamanca or Chueca.

Night Owls

Madrid's reputation as an all-night party town is deserved. Nightlife concentrates around Huertas, Lavapiés, Malasaña and off Sol. Gay-oriented Chueca is ultra cool and Salamanca is for a dressed-up occasion. But be warned: don't go out too early or you might think there is no action. A night out in Madrid can start at 10 or 11pm, after dinner, or even later, particularly on weekends and in the summer.

Flamenco show; musicians performing; flamenco dancer; taberna sign (top to bottom)

ESSENTIAL MADRID MADRID BY NIGHT

FLOODLIT STONE

Great cities look wonderful under floodlights and Madrid is no exception. Imaginative lighting enhances much of the city after dark. Don't miss the subtly lit charms of the Plaza Mayor, then enjoy the brilliance lighting adds to the Palacio Real and the Plaza de Oriente. The Paseo del Prado is beautifully illuminated at night; admire the sparkle of light on the water of the fountains in Plaza de Cibeles and Plaza de Canovas de Castillo before stopping at one of the summertime *terrazas*.

Eating Out

You can eat regional food from all over the peninsula in Madrid, as well as superb tapas, snacks and dishes from farther afield.

Where to Eat

There's a huge choice of eating places in Madrid, particularly around Sol, Santa Ana and Huertas, and the Latina, Lavapiés, Chueca and Malasaña districts. The city's smartest and priciest restaurants are concentrated near the Paseo del Prado and the Retiro and scattered throughout Salamanca. The IVA tax of seven per cent is added to bills in restaurants and bars. As for tipping, service is included; however it is customary to leave a few coins in a bar and five per cent in a restaurant.

Types of Restaurant

Restaurantes are officially graded with one to five forks, and range from simple establishments serving up the trusty *menú del día* to very grand—and pricey—venues. Tapas bars are quintessentially Spanish. These snacks range from a few olives or almonds to tortillas, shellfish, meat croquettes and wonderful vegetable dishes laced with garlic. All tapas bars have their own special dishes, and locals move from place to place, ordering the dishes that each bar does particularly well. The barman normally keeps track of what you've had to eat, and you pay at the end. The city has a very active café life, with some wonderful old places where you can read the papers and watch the world go by.

MEAL TIMES
The Spanish usually eat breakfast (*desayuno*) between 9 and 10, though it is served earlier in hotels. It's usually sweet—*chocolate con churros* (hot chocolate and stick-shaped doughnuts) or toast with jam. Traditionally, the main meal of the day, lunch (*almuerzo*) is from 2 to 4. The Spanish eat dinner (*cena*) any time after 9.30 through till midnight. But, with cafés and tapas bars open long hours, you can always find something tasty to eat.

Tapas bar; pinchos; taberna; tapas dishes (top to bottom)

ESSENTIAL MADRID EATING OUT

14

Restaurants by Cuisine

There are restaurants to suit all tastes and budgets in Madrid. On this page they are listed by cuisine. For a more detailed description of each restaurant, see Madrid by Area.

BASQUE AND CATALAN

Bokado (▷ 41)
Dantxari (▷ 41)
Errota-Zar (▷ 65)
Taberna del Alabardero (▷ 42)

COFFEE, TEA, CHOCOLATE AND ICE CREAM

Bajo Cero (▷ 94)
Chocolatería San Ginés (▷ 65)
La Esquina del Café (▷ 65)
Ritz Hotel (▷ 80)

GALICIAN AND ASTURIAN

A'Casiña (▷ 41)
Casa Mingo (▷ 41)
La Hoja (▷ 80)
Restaurante Moaña (▷ 66)
Taberna Maceira (▷ 66)

NATIONAL AND INTERNATIONAL

El 4 de Tapas (▷ 94)
Balzac (▷ 79)
La Castela (▷ 79)
La Gamella (▷ 79)

Indice Restaurant at AC Palacio del Retiro (▷ 80)
Nina Madrid (▷ 94)
Pedro Larumbe (▷ 94)
El Placer del Espíritu Santo (▷ 94)
Restaurante Viridiana (▷ 80)
La Sacristía (▷ 94)
Sula (▷ 80)
La Taquería de Birra (▷ 42)
Trattoria Sant'Arcangelo (▷ 80)

SPANISH

El Ingenio (▷ 41)
Mesón Cinco Jotas (▷ 42)
Prada a Tope (▷ 42)
Sal Gorda (▷ 42)
El Senador (▷ 42)
La Taurina (▷ 66)
Viuda de Vacas (▷ 66)

TAPAS

Baztán (▷ 94)
Los Caracoles (▷ 65)
Casa Alberto (▷ 65)
Casa Labra (▷ 65)
Cervecería Cervantes (▷ 65)
Lhardy (▷ 65)
Sanlúcar (▷ 42)
Taberna de Antonio Sánchez (▷ 66)
Vinoteca Barbechera (▷ 66)

TRADITIONAL MADRID CUISINE

La Bola Taberna (▷ 41)
Botín (▷ 65)
Café de Oriente (▷ 41)
El Molino de Los Porches (▷ 42)
Posada de la Villa (▷ 66)

If You Like...

Whatever your special interest while you are in Madrid, these suggestions should help you to make the most of your visit. Each sight or listing has more details later on in the book.

PEOPLE-WATCHING

Café de Oriente (▷ 41)**:** next to the Opera House, facing the Royal Palace.
Plaza Mayor: for architecture, murals, statues (▷ 51).
Retiro park lake: in a rowing boat (▷ 73).
Teleférico **(cable car):** on the way to or from the Casa de Campo (▷ 34).

SHOPPING TILL YOU DROP

ABC Serrano: a stylish indoor mall, with classy boutiques (▷ 92).
El Rastro: the fun Sunday morning market (▷ 53).
El Corte Inglés: Spain's top department store (▷ 61).
Mercado de Fuencarral: funky and fun (▷ 92).

Teleférico; shopping spree (above)

CHECKING OUT GREAT ART

The Prado: for Goya's greatest works (▷ 70).
Museo Nacional Reina Sofía: for Picasso's *Guernica* (▷ 46).
Museo Thyssen-Bornemisza: for 19th-century American art (▷ 48).

SPLASHING OUT

Genuine antiques: in the Galerías Piquér (▷ 62).
Fine ceramics: Antigua Casa Talavera (▷ 61).
A real fan: Casa de Diego (▷ 61).

The view of the Palacio de Cristál across the lake in El Retiro Park (above right); eye-catching fans (right)

Flamenco show (below)

BEING ENTERTAINED

Bullfighting: at the Plaza de Toros, the world's No.1 arena (▷ 98).

Flamenco: at a dozen clubs, such as Casa Patas (▷ 63).

Football: at Real Madrid (▷ 100), Atlético de Madrid, Rayo Vallecano.

Jazz: at the Café Central (▷ 63).

KEEPING KIDS HAPPY

Carriage ride: tour the city by night.

Casa de Campo: go to the Parque de Atracciones fairground (▷ 24).

Museo del Traje: dress up in 18th-century garb (▷ 31).

Playgrounds: let off steam in renovated plazas, such as the Plaza de Santa Ana (▷ 59).

KEEPING TO A TIGHT BUDGET

Concerts: check out free concerts in the Retiro park (▷ 73).

Festivals: ask at the tourist office if there are any parades or processions.

Free entry: visit museums on their weekly free entrance days.

Casa de Campo; flamingos in the zoo at Casa de Campo (above)

Museo de Escultura al Aire Libre: great sculpture free at the outdoor sculpture museum (▷ 89).

TRADITIONAL TAPAS

El 4 De Tapas (▷ 94).
Taberna de Antonio Sánchez (▷ 66).
Los Caracoles (▷ 65).

Selection of tapas (left)

OLD-FASHIONED FEASTING

Restaurante Botín; stay in a funky hotel (below)

Botín: the world's oldest restaurant (▷ 65).
Taberna Maceira: Galician cooking, especially *pulpo* (octopus) (▷ 66).
Restaurante Moaña: fish and seafood in a formal setting (▷ 66).
Posada de la Villa: traditional Madrid oven-roast lamb (▷ 66).

FUNKY HOTELS

Hospes: a new boutique hotel in a classic building (▷ 112).
ME Madrid: was the posh old Reina Victoria, now hip and happening (▷ 112).
Petit Palace: in the swish part of town, on top of the best window-shopping around (▷ 112).
Quo: a new group of funky hotels in the city (▷ 112).

CELEB-SPOTTING

La Bardemcilla (Augusto Figueroa 47), owned by film stars Monica and Javier Bardém.
Bar Skynight, on top of the Hotel Puerta América (Avenida de América) (▷ 112).
Fortuny, once a palace, still glitzy (▷ 93).
Glass Bar at the posh Hotel Urban (▷ 64).

Cocktails (above)

PARTYING TILL DAWN

Ojalá Awareness Club: the indoor beach is a must (▷ 93).
Café de la Palma: live music and DJs (▷ 40).
Kapital: seven floors of fun at Madrid's biggest club (▷ 79).

Dancing in a club (right)

Madrid by Area

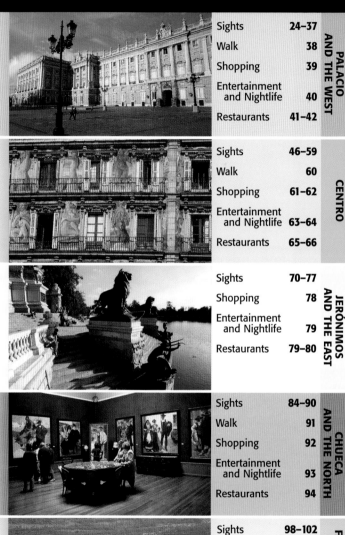

Sights	24–37
Walk	38
Shopping	39
Entertainment and Nightlife	40
Restaurants	41–42

PALACIO AND THE WEST

Sights	46–59
Walk	60
Shopping	61–62
Entertainment and Nightlife	63–64
Restaurants	65–66

CENTRO

Sights	70–77
Shopping	78
Entertainment and Nightlife	79
Restaurants	79–80

JERÓNIMOS AND THE EAST

Sights	84–90
Walk	91
Shopping	92
Entertainment and Nightlife	93
Restaurants	94

CHUECA AND THE NORTH

Sights	98–102
Excursions	103–106

FARTHER AFIELD

Palacio and the West

The Royal Palace is now a museum, but this area retains the elegance of the past. There are also plenty of green spaces.

Sights	24–37
Walk	38
Shopping	39
Entertainment and Nightlife	40
Restaurants	41–42

Top 25 **TOP 25**

Casa de Campo ▷ 24
Catedral de la Almudena ▷ 25
Ermita de San Antonio de la Florida ▷ 26
Monasterio de la Encarnación ▷ 27
Museo Cerralbo ▷ 28
Museo de América ▷ 30
Museo del Traje ▷ 31
Palacio Real ▷ 32
Parque del Oeste ▷ 34
Plaza de Oriente ▷ 35

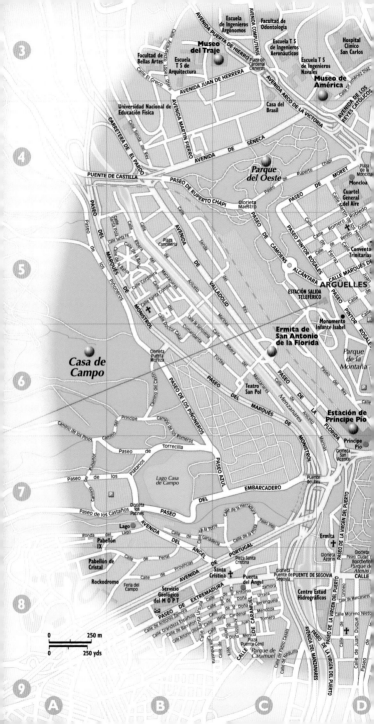

Plaza
Cristo Rey

CALLE ISAAC PERAL

CALLE LUCIANO Escava

CALLE DE Hilario Eslava

Arguelles
Mercado
URQUIJO CALLE ALBERTO AGUILERA
LA
Buen Suceso Quintana
Calle Calle
Francisco
Martín Calle Espíritu San Miguel
Calle del Rey Calle Calle Calle Fernando
PRINCESA

Servicio
Histórico
del Ejército
UNIVERSIDAD
Centro
Cultural
Conde
Duque
Ventura
Rodríguez
Plaza
Cristino
Martos

Templo de
Debod
Museo
Cerralbo
Torre de
Madrid
Plaza de los Reyes
Plaza de
España Plaza de
España
Monumento a
Cervantes
Calle
Plaza de
España
Calle de Tutor
GRAN
Calle de la Ilustración
Calle
Palacio
del Senado
VIA
Calle de Gonzalo
Santo
Domingo
CUESTA DE SAN VICENTE
Jardines
de Sabatini
Palacio
Real
BAILÉN Monasterio de la
Encarnación
Calle de Torija
Plaza de
Oriente
DE Calle de Arrieta
Calle de Vergara
Calle San Vicente
Opera/
Teatro
Real
Campo
del Moro
PALACIO
Plaza de
la Armería
CALLE Calle de Lepanto
Catedral
de la Almudena
San Nicolás
de los Servitas
BAILÉN
DE
Muralla
Árabe
Plasencia
Parque Emir
Mohamed I
DE SEGOVIA
metalúrgicos Viaducto
Calle de Beatriz Galindo
CALLE
Capilla
Cristo de
los Dolores
Plaza
G Miró
Plaza
Granado
Calle Redondilla
Calle Don Pedro
Calle de Mendizábal
Jardines de
las Vistillas
Plaza
San
Francisco
Basílica de
San Francisco
el Grande
GRAN VÍA DE SAN
Calle de Aljibe
Calle Ventosa
RONDA DE SEGOVIA
PASEO IMPERIAL
FRANCISCO

E   F   G

Casa de Campo

Flamingos in the zoo (left); running in Casa de Campo (right)

THE BASICS

🔲 A6
✉ Calle Marqués de Monistrol, Avenida de Portugal
🚇 Lago, Batán, Casa de Campo
🚌 25, 33, 65

Parque de Atracciones
www.parquedeatracciones.es
🔲 Off map at A7
☎ 91 463 29 00
🕐 Jun to mid-Sep daily noon–dusk; mid-Sep to Mar Sat–Sun noon–dusk; Easter week daily noon–dusk; Apr Fri–Sun noon–dusk; May Tue–Sun noon–dusk
🍴 Cafés, restaurants
🚇 Batán
🚌 33, 65 💷 Expensive

Zoo-Aquarium de Madrid
www.zoomadrid.com
🔲 Off map at A7
☎ 91 512 37 70
🕐 Mon Fri 11–dusk, Sat–Sun 10.30–dusk
🍴 Cafés, restaurants
🚇 Batán, Casa de Campo
🚌 33
💷 Expensive

TIP

● Take the 11-minute cable car trip from Parque del Oeste (▷ 34) for superb views over the city.

That Madrid is one of Europe's greenest capitals is mainly because of the 1,722ha (4,255-acre) Casa de Campo, 'the lungs of Madrid', stretching away to the northwest. Once a royal hunting estate, it was opened to the public in 1931, quickly becoming popular as a cool haven in Madrid's hot summer.

Wide open space In Casa de Campo, you can walk for a couple of hours without being interrupted (though this is best avoided after dark). During the Civil War, Franco's troops were based here, and signs of trenches are still visible. The park contains sports facilities, a large lake (where you can hire boats), amusement park, aquarium and zoo. The *teleférico* (cable car, www.teleferico.com) runs up here from the Parque del Oeste (▷ 34), and the 11-minute journey is an excellent way to arrive, affording superb views over the city.

Parque de Atracciones This amusement park has more than 40 rides, from gentle merry-go-rounds to the stomach-churning Top Spin and the breathtaking Tornado rollercoaster. There are open-air concerts in summer.

The zoo Madrid's zoo is one of the best in Europe. It contains over 5,000 animals and more than 100 species of bird, including 29 endangered species. There is a dolphinarium with twice-daily shows, a train ride, an aquarium and a children's section. Parrot shows, the tank of sharks and birds of prey are all popular.

Inside (left) the neo-classical Catedral de la Almudena (middle and right)

Catedral de la Almudena

Though not the loveliest cathedral, it reflects years of Spanish architectural thought. The mixture of styles shows how relaxed *madrileños* have been about this building, which you would expect to have been a priority.

A long delay Just 20 years ago, Madrid lacked a cathedral, incredible though it may seem. The first plans for the Almudena, constructed on what was formerly the site of Muslim Madrid's principal mosque, were drawn up in 1879 under Alfonso XII by the architect Giambattista Sacchetti. Redesigned in 1883, it is based on the pattern of a 13th-century cathedral, with a chancel similar to the one at Rheims. A neoclassical style was introduced into the design in 1944, but it wasn't until 1993, when the final touches were added, that the cathedral was consecrated by the Pope. The main entrance is opposite the Royal Palace, the entrance to the crypt along La Cuesta de la Vega.

The story of the Almudena Virgin According to legend, the image of the Virgin over the entrance had been hidden in the 11th century by Mozarabs. When Spanish hero El Cid reconquered Madrid, he ordered that the image be found, but without success. Alfonso VI then instructed his troops and the people of Madrid to dismantle the city walls to find the image. When they reached the grain deposits, they heard a noise from the turrets above, which then collapsed, revealing an image of the Virgin and Child.

THE BASICS

+ E7
✉ Calle Bailén. Next to Palacio Real
☎ 91 542 22 00
🕐 Daily 10–2, 5–8
Ⓜ Ópera
🚌 3, 31, 148
🎟 Free
♿ Good

HIGHLIGHTS

- Virgin of Almudena
- Coffin of San Isidro
- Dome 20m (66ft) in diameter
- Grenzing organ
- The 104m (340ft)-long nave
- 12 statues of the apostles
- Bronze doors

Ermita de San Antonio de la Florida

The façade of the hermitage (left); the exterior (right)

THE BASICS

www.munimadrid.es/ermita

⊞ C6

✉ Glorieta de San Antonio de la Florida 5

☎ 91 542 07 22

🕐 Tue–Fri 9.30–8, Sat, Sun 10–2. Closed public hols

Ⓜ Príncipe Pío

🚌 41, 46, 75

🚆 Norte Station

♿ None

💷 Free

HIGHLIGHTS

● Cupola
● Balustrade
● Marble and stucco font (1798)
● *Lápida de Goya*
● Mirrors under the cupola
● High altar
● Lamp under the cupola (18th century)
● *Inmaculada*, Jacinto Gómez Pastor
● *San Luis and San Isidro*, Jacinto Gómez Pastor

Goya is surely the painter that most *madrileños* want to claim as their own. The San Antonio de la Florida Hermitage, a National Monument, is a fine memorial to his memory.

Resting place Both church and hermitage—the latter to the left as you face the two buildings—are off the beaten track, but worthwhile both for their intimacy and to view Goya's frescoes. The original hermitage was begun in 1792 by Charles IV's Italian architect, Francisco Fontana. Goya's remains were buried here in 1919, but without his head: it is said that it was stolen by scientists who wished to study it.

The frescoes Painted using a technique that was revolutionary at the time, the frescoes are distinguished by their richness of colour. They tell the life of St. Anthony, representing the saint raising a murdered man from the dead to enable him to name his murderer and spare the life of the innocent accused. The models for the frescoes were members of the Spanish Court, but include other less reputable figures—placing rogues alongside the Court officials has been seen as indicating Goya's contempt for the Court of the time.

Girlfriends and boyfriends St. Anthony is the patron saint of sweethearts, and every 13 June girls come here to pray for a boyfriend. Thirteen pins are placed inside the font; then a girl puts her hand in and the number of pins that stick indicates how many beaux she will have that year.

The Monastery of the Incarnation (left); St. Teresa in stained glass (right)

Monasterio de la Encarnación

Located away from the traffic of Calle Bailén, the Monastery of the Incarnation is suffused with religious calm that brings peace to the soul.

History Designed by Juan Gómez de Mora in 1611 on instructions from Queen Margarita, wife of Philip III, the church in the Royal Monastery is typical of Habsburg Spanish religious architecture. Originally the monastery was connected by a passage to the Arab fortress where the Royal Palace now stands. The church was damaged by fire in 1734, and reconstructed in classical-baroque style; the granite façade is all that remains of the original. A 45-minute guided tour leads you through the monastery, which is still used by nuns of the Augustine order; you see the Royal Room, hung with uninspired portraits of the royal family, and one of Madrid's most beautiful churches, the monastery church, which includes a reliquary. Here, also, is the monastery museum.

The Reliquary In the middle of the church stands an altar and altarpiece depicting the Holy Family by Bernadino Luini, a pupil of Leonardo da Vinci, and an ornate tabernacle in bronze and rock crystal. Inside is a crucifix of Christ with a crown of thorns, oddly charred: tradition holds that these are the remains of a crucifix defiled by heretics. Among the 1,500 relics on display, in a small glass globe to the right of the door as you enter is the dried blood of St. Pantaleón, which is said to mysteriously liquify every year on 27 July, St. Pantaleón's Day.

THE BASICS

www.patrimonionacional.es

✚ E7

✉ Plaza de la Encarnación 1

☎ 91 454 88 00

◐ Monastery and Reliquary: Tue–Thu and Sat 10.30–12.45, 4–5.45, Fri 10.30–12.45, Sun 11–1.45

Ⓜ Ópera, Plaza de España

🚌 25, 39, 148

💶 Inexpensive. Free Wed for EU citizens

♿ None

HIGHLIGHTS

● *John the Baptist*, Jusepe Ribera
● *Handing over of the Princesses*, anonymous painting in lobby
● *Recumbent Christ*, Perronius
● Royal Room
● Altarpiece
● Cupola, with frescoes by González Velázquez
● Frescoes: Francisco Bayeu
● Charred crucifix
● Blood of St. Pantaleón

Museo Cerralbo

HIGHLIGHTS

- Grand staircase
- *Ecstasy of St. Francis*, El Greco
- *Jacob with his Flock*, José de Ribera
- *Devotion*, Alonso Cano
- *Immaculate Conception*, Francisco Zurbarán
- *Porcupines and Snakes*, Frans Snyders
- Sword collection from the courts of Louis XV and XVI
- Monumental mystery clock

TIP

- Check online if there is a free entry day.

Idiosyncratic and intermittently splendid, this curiosity shows you how the nobility of Madrid lived 100 years ago, in particular the extravagant and fascinating Marquis de Cerralbo.

Home life When you see the two-floor, late 19th-century home of the 17th Marquis of Cerralbo from the outside it looks rather unpromising. But the clutter of artefacts inside is fascinating, and, uniquely among the house-museums in Madrid, the collections are rivalled by the architecture and décor of the rooms themselves, ranging from the frankly shabby to the magnificent. Politician, man of letters and collector, the Marquis donated the house and its contents to the state in 1922, stipulating that his collection be displayed exactly as he had left it. This is a unique

The grand staircase (left); the mirrored ballroom (right)

opportunity to see a near-intact aristocrat's home of the turn of the 20th century.

The collection A magnificent grand staircase by Soriano Fort is to your right as you enter. On the second floor, the most notable exhibit is El Greco's striking *Ecstasy of St. Francis* (1600–05) in the chapel. In the gallery surrounding the patio, there are works by José de Ribera and Alonso Cano, as well as haunting Alessandro Magnasco landscapes. On the third floor there are collections of Western and oriental weaponry, a dining room containing a remarkable Frans Snyders painting, and an appealingly homey library. Pride of place is given to the sumptuous mirrored ballroom on the first floor, which displays the Marquis' Saxon porcelain, as well as intricate clocks, including one particularly fascinating and huge specimen.

THE BASICS

http://museocerralbo.mcu.es
➕ E6
✉ Calle Ventura Rodríguez 17
☎ 91 547 36 46
🕐 The museum was closed for restoration at time of writing and due to open at the end of 2009—check for times
🚇 Ventura Rodríguez, Plaza de España
🚌 1, 2, 44, 46, 74, 133, 202, circular
🎫 Inexpensive
♿ Few

Museo de América

TOP
25

An equestrian statue
set in the form of
a tree trunk (right)
at the American
Museum (left)

THE BASICS

www.museodeamerica.
mcu.es
✚ D3
✉ Avenida Reyes
Católicos 6
☎ 91 549 26 41
🕐 Tue–Sat 9.30–3, Sun
and public hols 10–3
Ⓜ Moncloa, Islas Filipinos
🚌 Circular, 1, 2, 16, 44, 46,
61, 82, 113, 132, 133
💶 Inexpensive. Free Sun
♿ Excellent

HIGHLIGHTS

● Canoe and tepee (Area 3)
● Statues of tribal chieftains
(Area 3)
● Painting of *Entrance of
Viceroy Morcillo into Potosí*
(Area 3)
● Shrunken heads (Area 4)
● Mummy of Parácas
(Area 4)
● Treasure of the Quimbayas
(Area 4)
● 'Day of the Dead'
paraphernalia (Area 4)
● Trocortesiano Maya Codex
(Area 5)

This attractive museum can be seen either as an attempt to promote international understanding or as propaganda for the Spanish Conquest. Still, it makes a unique contribution to Spanish culture.

History Devoted to the presentation and explication of pre-Columbian and Hispanic artefacts from Latin America, the America Museum, on the edge of the sprawling University area, is the best place in Spain to absorb the flavour of the culture of a different continent. Gold drew the Spanish to South America and gold draws visitors to marvel at the skills of the pre-Colombian artists. Many art works were melted down, so what is on show is even more important. Indeed, many South Americans living and working in Madrid are among the visitors. On Thursdays, the restaurant even serves an array of tasty South American dishes, such as *frijoles*, soups, Cuban-style rice and beans, green beans with tomatoes and spicy spaghetti.

Layout It's best to follow the suggested route, as it is easy to get confused. The collection is spread over two floors and five areas with different themes: the tools of understanding, the reality of America's society, religion and communication. Two particular highlights are the Treasure of the Quimbayas (Area 4), including exquisite gold figures, skull-cap helmets, drinking flasks and trumpets from Colombia, and the Trocortesiano Maya Codex (Area 5), which records the arrival of the Spaniards in the New World and the Spanish Conquest in minute, intricate runes.

One of the men's costumes on display (right) at the Museum of Costume (left)

Museo del Traje

Since its opening in 2004, the Museum of Costume has made its mark on the Madrid cultural stage. Far more than just clothes, the collection is a reflection of how Spanish society has changed over the centuries.

The collection In the 14 galleries of this elegant museum, the clothes are shown at different angles, so that you can see the front of some, the back of others. Through the glass, you can peer at centuries-old frock coats and silk doublets, and admire the embroidery on bodices. What you see is just a part of the collection that totals over 21,000 items. The galleries are organized chronologically, so that you can see how fashion and practicality evolved over centuries. The most delicate pieces are fragile and cannot be on display for long, so exhibits are routinely changed.

Hi-tech display Although historians are fascinated by the 13th-century trousseau of the daughter of Ferdinand III, most visitors are intrigued by a hi-tech display devoted to women's underwear. Virtual reality video twirls viewers from the bodices of the 17th century to the girdles of the 1940s. But there is everything in the museum, from Spanish *mantillas* to the latest shoes. Of course, with rooms all to themselves are Spain's legendary fashion designers, such as Mariano Fortuny (born in Granada) and Cristóbal Balenciaga, a Basque who went on to take the Parisian fashion world by storm. Best of all, you can try on old-fashioned clothes to get a feel of how comfortable—or uncomfortable—they were.

THE BASICS

www.museodeltraje.mcu.es
⊞ C3
⊠ Avenida Juan de Herrera 2
☎ 91 550 47 00
⏲ Tue–Sat 9.30–7, Sun and public hols 10–3
🍴 Café, restaurant
Ⓜ Moncloa, Ciudad Universitaria
🚌 46, 82, 83, 84, 132, 133
♿ Inexpensive. Free to under 18s, over 65s; Sat after 2.30, Sun
♿ Good

HIGHLIGHTS

● The funerary apparel of Doña María, daughter of Fernando III
● 1740s silver frock coat
● Women's underwear
● Spanish headdresses
● Regional costume
● The genius of Fortuny
● Christian Dior clothes
● Pedro Rodríguez and the New Look
● The catwalk

TIPS

● Book up for a special meal at Bokado (▷ 41), the museum's own very posh restaurant. In summer, dine out on the terrace.
● Excellent shop, with high-quality silk ties, Spanish shawls and jewellery.

Palacio Real

TOP 25

HIGHLIGHTS

● Grand staircase
● Sala de Porcelana
● Salón de Alabarderos
● Salón de Columnas
● Sala de Gasparini
● Salón de Carlos III
● Clock collection
● Chapel by Giambattista Sacchetti and Ventura Rodríguez
● Music Museum
● Sabatini Gardens

TIP

● The Changing of the Guard takes place at noon on the first Wed of the month (except Jul, Aug, Sep).

The scale of the palace is awesome and the pomp overwhelming. The story that sentries guarding the rear of the building used to freeze to death in the icy wind adds to the sense of chilliness it inspires.

Scaled to fit The Royal Palace was begun under Philip V in 1737, after the old Muslim fortress was destroyed by fire in 1734. The original design by Filippo Juvanna was for façades measuring 475m (520 yards) each, or three times longer than the palace now, but there was neither the space nor the money for that. It was completed in 1764, to designs by Sacchetti. From the street side, it is a normal palatial building of the period, with Doric pilasters framing the reception hall windows. The royal family does not actually live here: it is used occasionally for state visits, during which dinner is

The façade of the Palacio Real (left); statues lining the approach (middle); guards outside the palace (right); changing of the guard (bottom left); the exterior of the Royal Palace (bottom middle); a guard taking part in the changing of the guard ceremony (bottom right)

served in the gala dining room. The entrance is to the south side of the building, across the Plaza de la Armería, which is flanked by the Royal Armoury housing El Cid's sword and the ornate armour of Carlos V and Felipe III.

Interior and gardens There are more than 3,000 rooms, and most are never used. A ceiling by Conrado Giaquinto accents the grand staircase. The stucco ceiling of the Sala de Gasparini is remarkable, while the ceiling of the Sala de Porcelana, built for Charles III, has a fine display of white, gold and green porcelain plaques. To the north of the palace are the elegant Sabatini Gardens, which offer the best view of the palace, while to the rear is the Campo del Moro. The only way to see the palace is by following a fixed itinerary, which takes in the most impressive rooms.

THE BASICS

www.patrimonionacional.es
➕ E7
✉ Calle Bailén
☎ 91 454 88 00
🕐 Apr–Sep Mon–Sat 9–6, Sun and public hols 9–3; Oct–Mar Mon–Sat 9.30–5, Sun and public hols 9–3. Closed during public events
🚇 Ópera
🚌 3, 25, 39, 148
💷 Expensive. Free to under 5s; EU citizens on Wed
♿ Very good

Parque del Oeste

The rose garden (left); remains of the Templo de Debod (right)

THE BASICS

✚ C4
✉ Jardines del Paseo del Pintor Rosales
☎ 91 541 74 50
🕐 *Teleférico*: Sat, Sun and public hols 12–6
Ⓜ Argüelles
🚌 74, 84, 93

Templo de Debod
www.esmadrid.com
✉ Calle de Ferraz 1, Parque de la Montaña
☎ 91 366 74 15
🕐 Apr–Sep Tue–Fri 10–2, 6–8, Sat, Sun 10–2; Oct–Mar Tue–Fri 9.45–1.45, 4.15–6.15, Sat, Sun 10–2. Closed Mon and public hols
Ⓜ Plaza de España, Ventura Rodríguez
🚌 33, 39, 46, 74, 75, 148
🎫 Free

HIGHLIGHTS

● *Teleférico*
● La Rosaleda
● Fuente (fountain)
● Statue of Juan de Villanueva
● Statue of Sor Juana Inés de la Cruz
● Statue of Simón Bolívar
● View over Casa de Campo
● Trees, including atlas cedar, cypress and magnolia

Less frequented and more informal than the Retiro, the Parque del Oeste is the best place in the city for a peaceful stroll in summer, particularly at the quieter northern end. It is best avoided at night.

Rubbish dump to park Designed in the first years of the 20th century by landscape gardener Cecilio Rodríguez on what had previously been an immense rubbish heap, the Parque del Oeste was practically destroyed during the Civil War, when it provided a cover for the Republicans as the Nationalist troops invaded Madrid. Now rebuilt, it is still one of the city's most appealing and romantic open spaces. The park contains birch, fir, atlas cedar and cypress trees, among others, as well as a 17,000sq m (183,000sq ft) rose garden, La Rosaleda, which hosts a rose festival each May. The *teleférico* (cable car) in the park runs out to the Casa de Campo, affording bird's-eye views over the west of Madrid. In summer, elegant, noisy terrace bars are set up along the Paseo de Pintor Rosales, Ernest Hemingway's favourite street.

Templo de Debod It is somehow typical of Madrid that one of its most interesting attractions should not be Spanish at all. The Debod Temple, at the park's southern corner near Plaza de España, is a 4th-century BC Egyptian temple honouring the god Amon. It was installed in 1970 as a gift from the Egyptian government to Spanish engineers and archaeologists who had saved many treasures before large areas of land were flooded after the completion of the Aswan Dam.

Statues in the Plaza de Oriente, including an equestrian statue of Philip IV (middle)

Plaza de Oriente

Have an *aperitivo* on the terrace of the Café de Oriente, with the harmonious formal gardens stretching away in front of you to the Royal Palace. This is the place to reflect on the might of the monarchy at the height of its powers.

Ambitious emperor The elegant Plaza de Oriente was planned in 1811 under Joseph Bonaparte. To build it, he had to destroy the monuments and churches that then surrounded the Royal Palace. His original aim had been to build a kind of Champs-Élysées, running from the Plaza to the Cibeles Fountain. Fortunately, the Champs-Élysées project was abandoned; had it not been, Madrid would have lost, among many other treasures, the Monasterio de las Descalzas Reales (▷ 50; Convent of the Royal Shoeless Nuns). The existing square dates from the reign of Queen Isabella II (1833–1904). The attractively laid-out gardens contain statues of the kings and queens of Spain, which were originally intended for the top of the Royal Palace facing on to the plaza. They were never put into place because they were too heavy, and Isabella II dreamed that an earthquake made them topple over onto her.

Teatro Real At the eastern end of the square stands the Royal Theatre, built between 1818 and 1850 and now restored. The open-air building that originally occupied the site was expanded in 1737 for a visit by Farinelli, the legendary *castrato* singer, of whom Philip V (1683–1746) was particularly fond.

THE BASICS

- E7
- Plaza de Oriente
- Café de Oriente
- Ópera
- 25

HIGHLIGHT

● The equestrian statue in the middle of the square of Philip IV by Montañes, taken from a portrait by Velázquez

More to See

BASILICA DE SAN FRANCISCO EL GRANDE

Built between 1761 and 1784, this church has a neoclassical façade by Francisco Sabatini, one of the greatest practitioners of this style, and an overwhelming 33m (108ft) dome by Miguel Fernández. The monastery was used as a barracks from 1835, after which it was lavishly redecorated. The interior (note the ceiling frescoes) contains much work by Spanish masters, including an early Goya, *The Sermon of San Bernadino de Siena*, in the first chapel on the left. There is also a museum.

🖿 E8 ✉ Plaza de San Francisco, Calle de San Buenaventura 1 ☎ 91 365 38 00 🕒 Sep–Jul Tue–Fri 11–12.30, 4–6.30, Sat 11–1.30; Aug Tue–Sun 11–12.30, 5–7.30 🚇 La Latina 🚌 3, 60, 148 🚫 None 🖐 Inexpensive

CENTRO CULTURAL CONDE DUQUE

Madrid's municipal art centre is housed in an enormous 18th-century army barracks with a baroque façade. It includes a library, an auditorium and exhibition spaces but the principal attraction is the city's Museum of Contemporary Art, taking up two floors. Opened in 2001, the collection of 200 works by 177 artists is intended to complement, not compete with, Madrid's other art collections.

🖿 E5 ✉ Conde Duque 9/11 ☎ 91 588 57 63 🚇 Plaza de España, Noviciado 🚌 1, 2, 21, 44, 74, 133 🖐 Free

ESTACIÓN DE PRÍNCIPE PÍO

www.renfe.es

Restored and modernized, what was once the important Estación del Norte (North Station) is now both a busy commuter railway station for the suburbs and a lively destination shopping complex (▷ 39), with cinemas in the Centro de Ocio (leisure centre). There is also an important bus station outside what is still a handsome building, dating from the late 19th century. The station takes its name from Príncipe Pío, the nearby hill, where Spanish rebels were shot

A café on Plaza de España

by French soldiers on 3 May 1808.

➕ D6 ✉ Paseo de la Florida, corner of Cuesta de San Vicente 🚇 Metro Príncipe Pío 🚌 25, 33, 39, 41, 46, 75, 138

JARDINES DE LAS VISTILLAS

This park has wonderful views over the Casa de Campo towards the Guadarrama Mountains. A pleasant place for a relaxing drink.

➕ D8 ✉ Travesia Vistillas 🚇 Ópera, La Latina 🚌 3, 148

MURALLA ARABE

What little we can see of the Arab Wall is the oldest surviving part of Madrid. It was originally part of the walls of the small Arab town of Magerit. The area around it, now the Parque Emir Mohammed I, is one of the venues for the autumn arts festival.

➕ D8 ✉ Cuesta de la Vega 🚇 Ópera 🚌 3, 41, 148

PLAZA DE ESPAÑA

A statue of Cervantes stands at the western end of this grandiose square, overlooking a rather lovable 1815 statue of his two legendary creations, Don Quixote and Sancho Panza. On the edge of the square, with a neo-baroque doorway, is the Edificio España, Madrid's first true skyscraper, while the 137m (450ft) Torre Madrid was a symbol of post-Civil War economic recovery and Europe's tallest building when it was built in 1957.

➕ E6 ✉ Plaza de España 🚇 Plaza de España 🚌 68, 69, 74, 133

SAN NICOLÁS DE LOS SERVITAS

This is Madrid's oldest church and though much restored after the Civil War, its tower is one of the very few echoes of the Arabic Madrid in the city. Designated a National Monument, the tower is probably the minaret of a mosque later consecrated as a Catholic church. This 12th-century tower is Mudéjar (built by Muslims under Christian rule), while the central apse is Gothic.

➕ E7 ✉ Plaza de San Nicolás 6 ☎ 91 559 40 64 🕐 Mon 8.30–2, Sun 10–2, 6.30–8.30; do not visit during Mass. Not always open; advance phone call advisable 🚇 Ópera, Sol

Plaza de España

A Walk West from Sol

Stroll through some of Madrid's oldest streets and squares; take in the grandeur of the Palace and gardens.

DISTANCE: 5km (3 miles) **ALLOW:** 2–3 hours

START

PUERTA DEL SOL
⊞ F7 Ⓜ Puerta del Sol

END

ARGÜELLES
⊞ D5 Ⓜ Argüelles

① Leave the Puerta del Sol at the western end and take Calle de Postas up to Plaza Mayor. Cross the plaza and exit at the diagonally opposite corner (El Arco de los Cuchilleros).

② At the bottom of the steps cross the street and go down Calle del Maestro de la Villa and into the Plaza Conde de Barajas.

③ Cross the square, turn right on Calle del Conde Miranda, right again on Calle del Codo and into the Plaza de la Villa.

④ Cross Calle Mayor and follow Calle de los Señores de Luzon to the Plaza de Ramales. Cross the square and go downhill to Calle de Lepanto, which leads to the Plaza de Oriente.

⑦ Follow the path around to the right and continue up to the *Teleférico*. Take a ride for fantastic views or cross Paseo Pintor Rasales and walk up Calle de Marqués Urquijo to Argüelles Metro station.

⑥ Bear left, following the broad pavement to steps leading up the mound to the Templo de Debod. Walk past the temple to admire the views, descend the steps and turn right for the bandstand. Look down the hill to the Rosaleda rose garden.

⑤ Turn left and walk past the statues to the Palacio Real. Turn right and follow the promenade, walking along the Sabatini Gardens. Do not go down into the tunnel, but climb the steps on the left and continue across the bottom of the Plaza de España.

Shopping

BERBERÍA DEL SAHARA Y EL SAHEL

The name of this shop is a clue: come here for unusual and authentic materials and crafts from North Africa and the Sahara region. What makes it different is space devoted to exhibitions, travel guides and other information on the region.

🚇 E8 ✉ Redondilla 8
☎ 91 354 01 76
Ⓜ La Latina

CENTRO COMERCIAL PRÍNCIPE PÍO

www.ccprincipepio.com
This conversion of a railway station (the 1881 Estacíon del Norte) is a fine example of the imaginative recycling of old buildings that is going on in Madrid. Not far from the Royal Palace and the Catedral de la Almudena, find fashion in the basement and restaurants on the ground floor, as well as cinemas.

🚇 D6 ✉ Paseo de la Florida ☎ 91 758 00 40
Ⓜ Príncipe Pío

Some outstanding Spanish stores in this shopping complex include:

LURUEÑA

www.luruena.es
Leather in all shapes and sizes, from practical shoes and bags, to sandals and high heels. Men can find a full range, from formal office wear to casual vacation shoes; women have an even wider choice, with jazzy party bags and purses.

☎ 91 542 04 79

MASSIMO DUTTI WOMAN

www.massimodutti.com
This is an international Spanish company, despite its Italian name. Known for its classy style at mid-range prices, this store is devoted to women's clothing, as well as fragrances.

☎ 91 541 08 07

PULL & BEAR

www.pullbear.com
Appealing to the young market, this is another great Spanish fashion industry success story. Great fun, good prices.

☎ 91 542 06 91

SHOES

Thanks to its centuries-old leather industry, Spain has long had a love affair with *zapatos* (shoes). Many of the world's leading designers are Spanish, mainly from Alicante, Valencia and the Balearic Islands. They range from the extremely expensive (Loewe) to the extremely popular (Camper). And the choice for men's and children's shoes is almost as wide as for women's. Known for its outlet shops with bargain prices is Calle de Augusto Figueroa in Chueca.

TINO GONZÁLEZ

www.tinogonzalez.com
For imaginative yet practical shoes for men, women and children, Tino González has a wide range on offer, from formal to informal—and that special party pair.

☎ 91 632 44 90

TRUCCO

www.trucco.es
Rather than fashionistas, Trucco appeals to women with flair, who value attention to detail and quality. This is another popular and reliable Spanish-made international fashion franchise.

☎ 91 484 44 00

MUSEO DEL TRAJE

This museum (▷ 31) has one of the best gift shops around, with special emphasis on clothing, from Spanish *mantillas* to elegant silk ties, plus wonderful jewellery.

🚇 C3 ✉ 2 Avenida Juan de Herrera ☎ 91 550 47 00
Ⓜ Moncloa, Ciudad Universitaria

TONI MARTIN

www.tonimartindiscos.com
This music shop, specializing in country, jazz and rock 'n' roll, stocks a great selection of CDs and vinyl, new and second-hand.

🚇 E6 ✉ Calle Martin de los Heros 18 ☎ 91 542 50 20
Ⓜ Plaza de España

Entertainment and Nightlife

COPÉRNICO NOVA CLUB

Close to the university campus, this is the place to hear live bands from every part of the spectrum, from punk to metal. The décor is themed on a galleon, with telescopes and globes. Reasonable door charges.

➕ E4 ✉ Calle Fernández de los Ríos 67 ☎ 91 559 59 22 🕐 Nightly 11pm–6am 🚇 Moncloa

CORRAL DE LA MORERÍA

www.corraldelamoreria.com
A legendary flamenco *tablao*-restaurant which has been going strong for over 50 years. Open daily from 8pm, with two shows, each lasting an hour and a half, starting at 10pm and midnight. Reservation advised.

➕ E8 ✉ Calle de la Morería 17 ☎ 91 365 8446 🚇 Opera

ELANUET

For anyone young or old who reckons that music was better in the 1980s, this is the place to go for techno pop.

➕ E8 ✉ Calle Segovia 24 ☎ No phone 🕐 Wed–Sun 11pm–3.30am 🚇 La Latina

GOLEM CINE

www.golem.es
Until recently known as Alphaville, originally an art house cinema. Golem still shows international films in original versions with Soanish subtitles. There is

a good basement café.

➕ E6 ✉ Calle Martin de los Heros 14 ☎ 91 559 38 36 🕐 Check for times 🚇 Plaza de España

EL LIMBO

With clips from films projected onto screens, live bands and DJs, this is a popular venue with teenagers on a night out.

➕ E8 ✉ Calle Bailén 39 ☎ 91 365 21 58 🕐 Mon–Sat 10pm–3.30am 🚇 La Latina

MARULA CAFÉ

www.marulacafe.com
Soulfood sessions, funk and more at this popular club with live DJs. Cool bar, and an outdoor terrace in summer.

➕ E8 ✉ Calle Caños Viejos 3 ☎ 91 366 15 96 🕐 Mon–Sat 11pm–6am 🚇 La Latina

---

BOOM INDUSTRY

There are at least 60 cinemas in Madrid. Most have a discount day (Monday or Wednesday), when tickets are half price. Always arrive well in advance for evening weekend showings; queues can start forming an hour before projection time. Bigger cinemas now have advanced reservations and most have reserved seating on weekends. Movie information is published in full in all the daily newspapers: earliest showings (*pasos*) are generally at 4, latest at 10.30.

PRINCESA

Since it opened in the mid 1990s, this has become the city's main screening point for new Spanish films.

➕ E6 ✉ Calle Princesa 3 ☎ 91 542 11 72 🚇 Plaza de España

RENOIR

The best of the cinemas clustered around the bottom of Calle Martín de los Heros, near the Plaza de España, shows the latest art films. Detailed information sheets are published (in Spanish) to accompany each one. There are late showings on weekends.

➕ E6 ✉ Calle Martín de los Heros 12 ☎ 91 541 59 43 🚇 Plaza de España

STAR CAFÉ

Bands from Europe and the US perform rock and blues live Wed–Sat in this American-style café-bar, which serves hamburgers and french fries, ribs and pasta dishes. There is a good choice of beers and cocktails.

➕ D/E5 ✉ Calle Serrano Jovér 5 ☎ 91 542 28 17 🚇 Argüelles

TEATRO REAL

www.teatro-real.com
The grandest and most beautiful of the European opera houses.

➕ E7 ✉ Plaza de Isabel II ☎ 91 516 06 60/902 24 48 48 🚇 Ópera

Restaurants

PRICES

Prices are approximate, based on a 3-course meal for one person.

€€€   over €45
€€   €25–€45
€   under €25

A'CASIÑA (€€)

www.acasina.com
The Columnas, just one of the restaurant's large dining areas, is a sunlit indoor terrace overlooking the park. Start with *arroz caldoso con bogavante*, a rich lobster soup cooked with rice and follow up with the hake (*merluza*). Reservations essential.
B7/8 ⊠ Avenida de Angel, Casa de Campo ☎ 91 526 34 25 🅲 Closed Sun night 🚇 Lago

BOKADO (€€€)

www.bokadogrupo.com
With its cool modern interior and summer terrace, the Santamaría brothers' high-class Basque restaurant must be one of the world's best places to eat in a museum. In the Museo del Traje (▷ 31), book ahead for eye-catching Basque seafood treats.
C3 ⊠ Avenida de Juan de Herrera 2 ☎ 91 549 00 41 🅲 Closed Sun, Mon 🚇 Ciudad Universitaria, Moncloa

LA BOLA TABERNA (€€)

www.labola.es
La Bola is really an old tavern, boasting a century in business. It's best known for its *cocido madrileño* (a soup-style stew with noodles, chick-peas, meat and vegetables), presented in a sizzling pot. No credit cards.
E7 ⊠ Calle de la Bola 5 ☎ 91 547 69 30 🅲 Closed Sun night 🚇 Ópera, Santo Domingo

CAFÉ DE ORIENTE (€€€)

www.cafedeoriente.es
Built on the remains of a convent and facing the Royal Palace, this is a rather aristocratic place, with distinctive dishes that fuse *madrileño* with French cuisine.
E7 ⊠ Plaza de Oriente 2 ☎ 91 547 15 64/91 541 39 74 🚇 Ópera

REGIONAL CUISINE

Spanish regional cuisine—particularly that of the Basque country—has achieved greater international recognition than the cuisine of Madrid itself. Basque and Catalan cuisine tends to be fish-based, though if you do order meat, it is likely to come in the form of a huge steak. Basque tapas are available at some of the Basque restaurants; these are little culinary works of art. Galician specialties include seafood and hearty peasant dishes. The Asturians are known for their cider and *fabadas*, bean-based stews.

CASA MINGO (€)

www.casamingo.net
A popular Asturian *sidrería* or cider house. The idea is to pour the cider into the glass from a great height and drink it very fast. The best tapas are based on the strong Cabrales cheese. This restaurant is an excellent choice.
C6 ⊠ Paseo de la Florida 34 ☎ 91 547 79 18 🚇 Príncipe Pío

DANTXARI (€€–€€€)

www.dantxari.com
This Basque tavern offers spicy cod, and lamb with garlic and wild mushrooms. Wide-ranging Spanish wine list and cheerful service.
E6 ⊠ Ventura Rodriguez 8 ☎ 91 542 35 24 🅲 Lunch, dinner. Closed Sun, public hols 🚇 Ventura Rodríguez

EL INGENIO (€€)

www.restauranteingenio.com
This restaurant, close to Plaza Santo Domingo, serves traditional Spanish cuisine. You'll find salads, croquettes, wild mushrooms with aioli, vegetable stew, dried butterbean dishes and fresh cod on the menu. The place has a literary feel—Don Quixote paraphernalia adorn the walls. Reserving in advance is advisable, as it's a popular place.
E6 ⊠ Calle de Leganitos 10 ☎ 91 541 91 33 🅲 Closed Sun, public hols 🚇 Santo Domingo

41

MESÓN CINCO JOTAS (€€)

www.mesoncincojotas.com
One of a chain of well-run Cinco Jotas (5 Js) that pride themselves on serving the best quality (5 star, or 5 J) Iberian ham from Jabugo. Choose between the restaurant and the tapas bar.
🔢 E3 ⊠ Paseo de San Francisco de Sales 27 ☎ 91 544 01 89 ⊙ Daily 12.30–midnight, weekends till 1am 🚇 Islas Filipinas

EL MOLINO DE LOS PORCHES (€€€)

www.asadorelmolino.com
Join throngs of locals who come for *asado*, the roast meat that is both the house speciality and a Castilian speciality. Old-fashioned and proud of it. Popular summer garden dining. Important to book.
🔢 D5 ⊠ Paseo Pintor Rosales 1 ☎ 91 548 13 36 ⊙ Daily noon–midnight 🚇 Argüelles

PRADA A TOPE (€€)

www.pradaatope.es
Rustic and comfortable, this tavern is enhanced with aged-wood fittings. The cuisine is from León, which is known for its smoked beef, and this restaurant does it proud. *Cocido*, *tortilla*, roast beef and spicy green peppers are all on the menu. Two branches in Madrid.
🔢 D7 ⊠ Cuesta de San Vicente 32 ☎ 91 559 39 53 ⊙ Closed Tue 🚇 Plaza de España, Príncipe Pío

Also: 🔢 G7 ⊠ Príncipe 11 ☎ 91 429 59 21 ⊙ Closed Sun dinner, Mon 🚇 Sevilla

SAL GORDA (€€)

This long-established restaurant is off the beaten tourist trail and popular with locals for its dishes: Spanish through and through. Excellent value for money.
🔢 E2 ⊠ Beatriz de Bobadilla 9 ☎ 91 553 95 06 ⊙ Closed Sun, Aug 🚇 Guzmán el Bueno

SANLÚCAR (€)

www.barsanlucar.tk
A classic Andalucian-style tapas bar with owners from Cadiz, so sherries are the perfect accompaniment for prawns, *langostinos* (crayfish) and other seafood. Well-priced three-course menu of the day.
🔢 E8 ⊠ San Isidro Labrador 14 ☎ 91 354 00 52 ⊙ Closed Sun dinner, Mon 🚇 La Latina

REGIONAL FARE

After the Basques, the Galicians have the best cuisine in Spain. Together with their neighbours the Asturians, they prefer maritime cuisine, and the portions are generally sizeable, with potatoes the staple food. Regional special dishes include *pulpo* (octopus), and *pimientos de Padrón* (hot green peppers)—best eaten with a jug of water.

EL SENADOR (€€)

www.restaurantesenador.com
This well-established traditional restaurant serves Segovian cuisine. The house special is roast lamb, but there are also steaks cooked on a charcoal fire and fresh fish. The wine is great, and so are the desserts. Tapas are available at the bar. Reserve in advance.
🔢 E7 ⊠ Plaza de la Marina Española 2 ☎ 91 541 22 21 ⊙ Closed Sun night 🚇 Santo Domingo, Ópera

TABERNA DEL ALABARDERO (€€€)

www.alabardero.com
A plush restaurant next to the Teatro Real named after the soldiers of the king's bodyguard. You're likely to rub shoulders with politicians, bullfighters and literary figures here. If you can't afford the price of a meal you can still have excellent tapas at one of the bar's terrace tables.
🔢 E7 ⊠ Felive V 6 ☎ 91 547 25 77 ⊙ Daily 🚇 Ópera

LA TAQUERÍA DE BIRRA (€)

www.lastaquerias.com
Where locals come to get their fill of Mexican dishes, such as tacos (including vegetarian tacos). Jolly atmosphere, with Mexican music.
🔢 E8 ⊠ Don Pedro 11 ☎ 91 366 45 39 ⊙ Daily 7.30–2.30am; weekends, public hols 1pm–2.30am 🚇 Ópera

This is the Madrid that most visitors expect to see: medieval lanes, great art museums, tapas bars on every corner. It's best explored on foot.

Sights	46–59
Walk	60
Shopping	61–62
Entertainment and Nightlife	63–64
Restaurants	65–66

Top 25

Museo Nacional Reina Sofía ▷ 47
Museo Thyssen-Bornemisza ▷ 48
Monasterio de las Descalzas Reales ▷ 50
Plaza Mayor ▷ 51
Puerta del Sol ▷ 52
El Rastro ▷ 53
Real Academia de Bellas Artes ▷ 54

CAFETERÍA
RESTAURAN
FREIDURÍ

The museum's glass elevators (opposite, left and right); Picasso's Guernica *(middle)*

Museo Nacional Reina Sofía

CENTRO

TOP 25

In Madrid's leading modern art museum, the home of Picasso's *Guernica*, you might not like all the works on display. But even on its busiest days, the light and airy space is a delight.

A triumph of planning Inspired by the Pompidou Centre in Paris, this 12,540sq m (135,000sq ft) space is Madrid's finest contemporary art museum; among European museums only the Pompidou is larger. It occupies a building that served as the San Carlos hospital between 1977 and 1986. Transparent elevators on the outside whisk you up for a thrilling view over the rooftops of Madrid. The fine permanent collection showcases Spanish art of the 20th century—cubism, surrealism, realism, informalism. The dramatic extension by French architect Jean Nouvel opened in 2004. Under the red roof are galleries for temporary exhibitions, as well as the library, shop, café and auditorium.

Guernica Picasso's masterpiece dominates the Reina Sofía. When it was commissioned by the Republican Government for display at the 1937 Paris Exhibition, the only instruction was that it be big: it measures 6.4 x 7m (21 x 23ft). Taking his inspiration from the Nationalist bombing of the Basque town of Guernica in 1937, this painting has become 20th-century art's great anti-war symbol. Many saw the 1995 decision to remove the bullet-proof screen that had protected it for many years as a symbolic gesture, showing that democracy in Spain had finally taken root.

THE BASICS

www.museoreinasofia.es
🚼 G9
✉ Calle Santa Isabel 52
☎ 91 774 10 00
🕐 Mon, Wed–Sat 10–9, Sun 10–2.30
🍴 Bar, restaurant
Ⓜ Atocha
🚌 6, 10, 14, 24, 26, 27, 32, 34, 36, 37, 41, 45, 47, 55, 57, 85, 86
🚉 Atocha
💰 Moderate. Free to under 18s, over 65s; Sat afternoon and Sun
♿ Very good

HIGHLIGHTS

● View from exterior elevators
● Enclosed patio
● *Guernica*, Picasso
● Joan Gris Room
● Picasso Room
● Joan Miró Room
● Dalí Room
● Surrealism Room
● Luis Buñuel Room
● Spanish 20th-Century Art Room

Museo Thyssen-Bornemisza

HIGHLIGHTS

● *Portrait of Giovanna Tornabuoni*, Domenico Ghirlandaio
● *Portrait of Henry VIII*, Holbein
● *St. Catherine of Alexandria*, Caravaggio
● *Annunciation Diptych*, Van Eyck
● *St. Jerome in the Wilderness*, Titian
● *The Lock*, Constable
● *Easter Morning*, Caspar David Friedrich
● *Les Vessenots*, Van Gogh
● *Man with a Clarinet*, Picasso

TIP

● In summer, the rooftop terrace is open for romantic dinners. Also in summer, the museum is open on Monday, and late at night.

This is one of the best things that has happened to Madrid since the end of the Civil War. It is also one of the few internationally renowned art museums where everything is priority viewing.

New museum The collection was begun by the German financier and industrialist Baron Heinrich Thyssen-Bornemisza in the 1920s and continued after his death by his son, Hans Heinrich (who died in 2002). The 775 paintings exhibited here were sold to the Spanish state for a mere $350 million in 1993, one year after the museum opened to the public. The permanent collection, spanning seven centuries, is housed in the sympathetically renovated 18th-century Palacio de Villahermosa. In 2004, the glass pavilion opened. It contains 19th- and 20th-century paintings from

The museum's entrance hall (left); gallery displaying 20th-century art (right)

CENTRO

★

TOP 25

the collection of Hans Heinrich's widow, Carmen Thyssen-Bornemisza, a former Miss Spain.

The collection The sheer variety of the many works on display prompted some to call the Thyssen over-eclectic; others claim its very quirkiness is part of its charm. Each room highlights a different period: the top floor is devoted to art from medieval times through to the 17th century; the second floor to rococo and neoclassicism of the 18th and 19th centuries through to fauvism and expressionism; the first level to 20th-century surrealism, pop art and the avant-garde. Start from the top and work your way down. It is worth renting an audio guide, available in Spanish, English, French, German and Italian. The museum's shop is one of the best, whether you are looking for art books or beautiful gifts.

THE BASICS

www.museothyssen.org

🕂 G7

✉ Paseo del Prado 8

☎ 91 369 01 51

🕐 Tue–Sun 10–7

🍴 Café, restaurant

Ⓜ Banco de España

🚌 1, 2, 5, 9, 10, 14, 15, 20, 27, 34, 37, 45, 51, 52, 53, 74, 146, 150

🚆 Atocha, Recoletos

💰 Moderate. Free to children under 12; reduction to over 65s

❓ Bookstore on the ground floor

♿ Excellent

Monasterio de las Descalzas Reales

Marble tomb of the Empress Maria (left) at the Monasterio de las Descalzas Reales (right)

HIGHLIGHTS

● *Recumbent Christ*, Gaspar Becerra
● *Neapolitan Nativity* (Chapel of St. Michael)
● *Bust of the Mater Dolorosa*, José Risueño
● *Cardinal Infante Don Fernando of Austria*, Rubens
● *The Ship of the Church*, 16th-century painting
● *Adoration of the Magi*, Brueghel
● *The Empress María*, Goya
● *17th-century tapestries*

Though the tour of the Royal Shoeless Nuns' Convent is conducted at a brisk pace, the building contains an unusually high proportion of unmissable treasures.

Convent history Of Madrid's two monastery museums, the Descalzas Reales is the richer; most of its rooms are small museums in themselves. Founded by Juana of Austria, the younger daughter of Charles V, on the site of the place in which she was born, it was built between 1559 and 1564 in Madrid brick by Antonio Silla and Juan Bautista of Toledo. The whole place breathes mid-17th-century religious mysticism, though the 'vile stink' of which traveller William Beckford complained when attending Mass in the late 18th century has departed. The original sisters were all of noble or aristocratic blood, and each founded a chapel on reception into the order: there are 33 of them, and to this day the convent is home to 23 Franciscan nuns, each of whom maintains one of the chapels. The Grand Staircase, with its *trompe l'oeil* portrait of Philip IV and his family standing on the balcony, is covered with frescoes by the artist Claudio Coello. With its incongruous location right in the middle of commercial Madrid, it is a small miracle that it remains intact.

Seeing the collection The only way to see the convent is to take a tour. Given in Spanish only, it lasts around 45 minutes and is conducted at such a frenzied pace that it is worth buying a guide book at the entrance. The church can be visited only during Mass, at 8am or 7pm.

Views of the Casa de Panadería on Plaza Mayor

Plaza Mayor

The cobbled Plaza Mayor strikes a chord with everyone entering it for the first time: it's here that you fully realize you are in the capital of Spain.

Work in progress Built in the 15th century as a market square, and later renamed the Plaza del Arrabal (Square outside the Walls), the Plaza Mayor came into its own when Philip II, after making Madrid the capital of Spain, ordered it rebuilt as the administrative centre of the Court. The only part to be completed immediately was the Panadería, or the bakery, by architect Diego Sillero in 1590 (the frescoes are the work of the early 1990s), while the rest of it was completed in 1619 by Juan Gómez de la Mora under Philip III, whose bronze statue stands in the middle. After a fire in 1790, much of the square had to be rebuilt. The buildings between the towers on either side are Town Hall offices; the rest are private homes. The 18th-century Arco de los Cuchilleros, leading from the square into Cava Baja, is named after the cutlers who once worked here making knives for local butchers and swords for the nobility.

A gathering place The Plaza Mayor was where the more important members of the Court lived during the 17th century; at the end of the century, the square became the site of mounted bullfights, carnivals and the terrible *autos da fé* of the Spanish Inquisition, attended by thousands on 30 June 1680, when 118 offenders were executed in a single day. Hangings were also carried out here until the end of the 18th century.

THE BASICS

➕ F7/8
✉ Plaza Mayor
🍴 *Terraza* bars around square
🚇 Sol, Ópera
🚌 3, 17, 18, 23, 31, 35
❓ Tourist office in square

TIPS

● In May, free concerts are held during the 2 May and San Isidro festivities.
● The plaza hosts the city's annual Christmas market.

CENTRO

TOP 25

51

Puerta del Sol

The bear and tree, symbol of Madrid (left); statue of Carlos III (middle and right)

THE BASICS

➕ F7

✉ Puerta del Sol

🚇 Sol

🚌 3, 5, 15, 20, 51, 52, 150

HIGHLIGHTS

● Bear and *madroño* (strawberry tree) statue
● Statue of Charles III
● La Mallorquina pastry shop
● Newspaper stands: a major part of Madrid streetlife
● Tio Pepe sign
● Kilometre Zero
● Doña Manolita's lottery ticket kiosk

Almost inevitably, you will cross this square several times. For many *madrileños*, it is the true soul of the city and each year thousands gather here to see in the New Year.

Soul of Madrid The area's namesake gateway was demolished in 1570 when the square was widened to receive Anne of Austria, Philip II's fourth wife. The design of the present square dates back to 1861; the building on the south side, the Casa de Correos, is from 1768. Originally the Post Office, it is now the headquarters of the Madrid regional government. Spain's Kilometre Zero, the point from which all distances in Spain are measured, can be found on the pavement in front of it. The clock and tower were built in 1867.

A troubled past The Esquilache mutiny of 1766 began here, sparked by Charles III's uncharacteristically tyrannical insistence that the population should wear short capes and three-cornered hats to emulate a hated French style. The most notable moment in Sol's history was on 2 and 3 May 1808, when *madrileños* took up arms against occupying French troops, a heroic resistance in which more than 2,000 died, immortalized in Goya's two magnificent anti-war paintings in the Prado, *Dos de Mayo* and *Tres de Mayo*. It was here, also, that politician José Canalejas was assassinated in 1912, and the Second Republic was proclaimed in 1931. It remains a popular meeting place, especially by the monument of the bear with a strawberry tree, the symbol of Madrid.

Grab a bargain at El Rastro market

El Rastro

www.elrastro.org

☐ F9

✉ Ribera de Curtidores

🕐 9–3

🍴 Many cafés and bars

Ⓜ Tirso de Molina

HIGHLIGHTS

● Street vendors shouting
● Spanish pottery
● Antiques at Galerías Piquer
● Leather boots and saddles at Curtidos Roman, Calle Ribera de Curtidores 16

For locals and visitors alike, this is the classic place to spend a Sunday morning. The Rastro is much more than a flea market; crowds bustle as if they are off to a football match. Be careful with your valuables.

Bargains galore Start from the Tirso de Molina Metro station, and head for the Plaza de Cascorro. The lines of stalls run downhill, along both sides and in the middle of the Ribera de Curtidores street, and go on to form a busy triangle with Calle de Toledo and Calle Embajadores. It all gets under way at 9am, and the trick is to take your time and to tuck all your valuables away. Bargains are here for those who poke, prod and haggle for old birdcages and cheap underwear, leather bags and clay pots.

A bloody history But it is not just the main street. All the regular shops are open, and the market spills into the side streets. Find pets on Calle de Fray Ceferino González, and every sort of painting, from watercolours and prints to original oils, on the Calle de San Cayetano, nicknamed the Painters' Street. Drop by the Galerías Piquér (▷ 62), a courtyard surrounded by antiques shops. As for the name, *rastro* dates back to the 16th century, when this was the site of a slaughterhouse. When the dead animals were dragged away to the tanners (*curtidores*), they left a *rastro*, trail of blood on the street.

CENTRO

TOP 25

Real Academia de Bellas Artes

HIGHLIGHTS

● Goya self-portraits (Room 20)
● *The Burial of the Sardine*, Goya (Room 20)
● *Alonso Rodríguez*, Francisco Zurbarán (Room 6)
● *Head of John the Baptist*, José de Ribera (Room 3)
● *Felipe IV*, Velázquez (Room 11)
● *Susana and the Elders*, Rubens (Room 13)
● *Spring*, Giuseppe Arcimboldo (Room 14)
● Goya etchings (Calcografía Nacional)

TIP

● Don't miss the Calcografía Nacional, with its room dedicated to Goya's disturbing engravings.

The Prado, Thyssen and Reina Sofía may have more visitors, but the eclectic collections of the Royal Academy of Fine Arts, the oldest permanent art institution in Madrid, are interesting to see.

History It was Francisco Meléndez who suggested the establishment of a Royal Academy on the model of those in Rome, Paris, Florence and other great cities. Work began on the authorization of Philip V in 1744 and was completed under Fernando VI in 1752. The Academy was initially in the Casa de la Panadería, in the Plaza Mayor, but Charles III transferred it to its present site in 1773. The original building was baroque, but shortly after it opened, Academy members with conservative tastes insisted that it be given today's neoclassical façade. Rarely overcrowded,

Alonso Rodríguez, *by Francisco Zurbarán, (left) on display at the Royal Academy of Fine Arts (right)*

it is small enough to be visited comfortably in a couple of hours.

Layout The museum has three floors. The best-known galleries are on the second floor, most notably Room 20, with its Goyas. Other highlights by 17th-century Spanish artists include *Head of John the Baptist* by José de Ribera (1591–1652), *Alonso Rodríguez* by Francisco Zurbarán, and *Felipé IV* by Velázquez. *Spring,* by the 16th-century Milanese painter Giuseppe Arcimboldo, in Room 14, is the only Arcimboldo in Spain and one of only a handful in the world. Halfway up the stairs to the entrance (and easily missed) is another museum, La Calcografía Nacional, or Engraving Plates Museum. The Gabinete Goya at the back of this contains a beautifully displayed series of the original plates used by the artist for his etchings.

THE BASICS

http://rabasf.insde.es
✚ G7
✉ Calle de Alcalá 13
☎ 91 524 08 64
🕐 Tue–Fri 9–7, Sat–Mon and public hols 9–2.30
🚇 Sol, Sevilla
🚌 3, 5, 15, 20, 51, 52, 53, 150
💷 Inexpensive. Free to under 18s, over 65s; Wed
♿ Limited

More to See

CAIXAFORUM

www.obrasocial.lacaixa.es

This exhibition space and concert hall is an extraordinary piece of architecture. What was a power station now has an alien, upward extension sprouting from its roof and a deep porch, making it look as if the mass above is hovering above the ground. What would otherwise be an ugly bare wall in front of the entrance has been transformed into a 'vertical garden', a mass of dripping greenery.

H8 ⬛ Paseo del Prado 36 Ⓜ Atocha
🚌 6, 10, 14, 26, 27, 32, 34, 37, 45
💷 Free, occasional charge for certain concerts

CALLE MAYOR

This is perhaps the most traditional of Madrid's streets, with some old-fashioned shops—including a wonderful *guitarrería* (guitar store) near the Calle Bailén end. Spain's two greatest playwrights, Lope de Vega and Calderón de la Barca, lived at Nos. 25 and 61 respectively.

E/F7 Ⓜ Sol 🚌 3

CALLE DEL MESÓN DE PAREDES

To get a complete sense of the slightly surreal and multicultural atmosphere of Madrid's *barrio popular*, stroll down this street and those around it on any weekday morning, when it is bustling and full of life. La Corrala is an 1882 example of the corridor-tenement found throughout working-class Madrid. From the early 1980s, it was used for productions as an open-air theatre. It is now an Artistic Monument. The Taberna de Antonio Sánchez at No 13 (▷ 66) is one of the best-preserved examples of Madrid's traditional 19th-century bars, or *tabernas*. A few others still survive around the old parts of the city, some of them still with their original tile work, marble-topped tables and polished zinc counters.

F9 Ⓜ Tirso de Molina, Lavapies
🚌 32, 57

CASA MUSEO LOPE DE VEGA

Spain's greatest playwright, Felix Lope de Vega (1562–1635), lived in this

Gran Vía

house from 1610 until his death. Now an evocative museum, the rooms are furnished in the style of the period, based on an inventory by Lope himself. There are lovely gardens behind this museum, which is located just uphill from the Paseo.

➕ G8 ✉ Calle de Cervantes 11 ☎ 91 429 92 16 🕐 Tue–Fri 9.30–2, Sat 10–2. Closed public hols, Aug 🚇 Banco de España, Antón Martín 🚌 On Paseo del Prado 👐 Free

COLEGIATA DE SAN ISIDRO

San Isidro is the patron saint of Madrid and, between 1885 and 1993, until the completion of the Almudena (▷ 25), this immense baroque church was Madrid's unofficial cathedral. Built in 1620 by Pedro Sánchez for the Jesuits, the church was commandeered by Charles III after he expelled them. San Isidro's remains, until then in San Andrés, were brought here at that time.

➕ F8 ✉ Calle Toledo 37–39 ☎ 91 420 17 82 🕐 Daily 7.30–1.30, 6–9. Closed during services 🚇 La Latina 🚌 17, 23, 35 ♿ None 👐 Free

GRAN VÍA

Running between the Calle de Alcalá and the Plaza de España, the imposingly massive Gran Vía is one of the city's great axes; with its shops and cinemas, it is very lively and stimulating for early evening strolls. Begun in 1910 under Alfonso XII, it led to the shortening or destruction of 54 other streets.

Serving as Madrid's great northern axis, the road peels off from Calle de Alcalá a short way from Plaza de Cibeles. It was conceived in the late 19th century as a way to allow Madrid to expand. Work finally began in 1910, with the last stretch completed in 1929. The building of this thoroughfare provided an opportunity for architects of the early 20th century to apply new styles. The best are at the start of the street, on or near the junction of Alcalá and the Gran Vía. The most striking building is the Edificio Metropolis, which was finished in 1911. Its slate dome is ornamented with gold and topped by a winged statue of Victory. Next to it is No. 1 Gran Vía, the Edificio Grassy (1917), named after the jeweller's shop in the

A portrait of Lope de Vega at his former home, Casa Museo Lope de Vega

Theatre on the Gran Vía

ground floor and distinguished by its colonnaded tower. Moving up the street, on the north side (No. 12) is a 1931 art deco cocktail bar, Museo Chicote, made famous by its association with author Ernest Hemingway and the Hollywood actress Ava Gardner. Don't miss the Telefonica building (No. 28), a Manhattan-style skyscraper, the tallest building in Madrid when it was erected in 1929.
✚ F/G7 🚇 Gran Vía, Callao 🚌 44, 46, 74, 133, 146, 147, 148, 149

PLAZA DEL CONDE DE BARAJAS

Looking for a special souvenir of Madrid? Visit this delightful spot on a Sunday, when artists set up their stalls to sell oil paintings and watercolours. Prices range from cheap to unbelievable, but it is worth haggling. At Christmas, concerts and flamenco dancing events are also held here. It's located southwest of the Plaza Mayor between Calle de la Pasa and the Pasadizo del Panecillo.
✚ E8 🚇 La Latína

PLAZA DE LAS CORTES

www.congreso.es

This is the home of the Congreso de los Diputados, or parliament buildings. The ceremonial entrance to the parliament is guarded by two bronze lions popularly known as Daoíz and Velarde after the heroic captains of the Napoleonic invasion. An attempted military coup took place inside the building in 1981, and was recorded on video for posterity. There are weekly guided tours. In the middle of the square stands a statue of Spain's most famous author, Miguel de Cervantes, renowned for his novel *Don Quixote*.
✚ G7 ✉ Plaza de las Cortes 🚇 Sevilla 🚌 5, 150, N5, N6

PLAZA DE LA PAJA

During Muslim rule, this pleasant little Straw Square was the site of the city's most important *zoco*, or street market; during the Middle Ages it housed aristocratic residences. Of the many palaces located here, the most notable is at No. 14, the Lasso de Castilla, the

Congreso de los Diputados on Plaza de las Cortes

An outdoor café on Plaza de la Paja

preferred residence of Catholic kings when they stayed in Madrid, sadly now extremely unpalatial in appearance.

🕇 E8 ✉ Plaza de la Paja 🚇 La Latina 🚌 3, 31, 148

PLAZA DE SANTA ANA

Once occupied by the Santa Ana monastery, which was torn down during Joseph Bonaparte's rule (1808–13), the refurbished plaza is surrounded by bars and is perfect for people-watching in summer. The square is home to the oldest theatre in Madrid, Teatro Español, which was built in 1745 and puts on classical Spanish productions.

🕇 F8 ✉ Plaza de Santa Ana 🚇 Sol, Sevilla 🚌 5, 150

PLAZA DE LA VILLA

With its small scale, this rectangular and typically Castilian square makes a pleasant change from some of the more imposing buildings in Madrid. Originally the site of an Arab street market, it is now home to three buildings in three distinct styles:

the Castilian-baroque Ayuntamiento, the Casa de la Villa, designed in 1630 by Juan Gómez de Mora; the much-restored Casa de Cisneros, on the south side of the square, one of Madrid's finest examples of the plateresque style prevalent in the 16th century; and the Torre de los Lujanes, one of the few surviving monuments from the 15th century.

🕇 E8 ✉ Plaza de la Villa 🚇 Sol, Ópera 🚌 3

SAN PEDRO EL VIEJO

Noteworthy principally for its 14th-century Mudéjar tower and the legends surrounding it, San Pedro stands on the site of an old mosque. In the doorway are the only coats of arms extant from the period preceding the Catholic monarchs. Part of the interior dates from the 15th century, while the rest is largely of 18th-century construction.

🕇 E8 ✉ Costanilla de San Pedro ☎ 91 365 12 84 🕐 Daily 6–8pm; do not visit during Mass 🚇 La Latina, Tirso de Molina ♿ None

Casa de Guadalajara on Plaza de Santa Ana

A Walk East from Sol

Take this walk to see the Spanish parliament and the Prado, the Botanic Gardens and Retiro Park.

DISTANCE: 6.7km (4 miles) **ALLOW:** 2–3 hours

❶ Start on the Puerta del Sol. Exit at its eastern end and walk down Calle de San Jerónimo, all the way to the Plaza de las Cortes. Continue past the south side of the Museo Thyssen-Bornemisza to the Plaza de Cánovas de Castillo.

❼ Continue past the Plaza de las Silesa and turn sharp left down Calle de Barquillo. Follow this all the way down to Calle de Alcalá.

❻ At the Plaza de Colón, turn left on Paseo de Recoletos. Cross over at the entrance to Recoletos station. On the west side of the Paseo, turn right on Calle Bárbara de Braganza.

❷ Turn right down the Paseo del Prado and cross at Plaza de la Platería de Martínez. Visit the Jardín Botánico, on the south side of the Prado. Or continue along Calle de Espalter to Calle de Moreto.

❺ At the fountain, bear left for the Puerta de Alcalá, cross Calle de Alcalá, and walk up Calle de Serrano. Pass the Archaeological Museum and turn left on Calle de Jorge Juan.

❸ Turn left and walk uphill, past San Jerónimo del Real, to Calle de Félipe IV. Turn right, walk up past the Casón del Buen Retiro, cross Calle de Alfonso XII and enter the Retiro Park.

❹ Stroll through the parterre gardens and up the steps at the end. When you reach the lake, turn left and follow its edge. Across the water is the dramatic Alfonso XII monument.

Shopping

AMPARO MERCERÍA

As this grand old haberdashery store confirms, stitching and mending, sewing and knitting are still popular skills in Spain. Founded back in 1861, the store retains that sense of history with a solid wooden counter, as well as selections of buttons, needles, sequins and lace.
🔲 F7 ✉ Calle Marqués Viudo de Pontejos 5 ☎ 91 522 52 97 🔘 Sol

ANTIGUA CASA TALAVERA

For fine hand-painted ceramics from Talavera, Granada and Toledo. This 100-year-old establishment has both original and reproduction vases and platters with patterns that go back 1,000 years.
🔲 E7 ✉ Calle de Isabel la Católica 2 ☎ 91 547 34 17 🔘 Santo Domingo

ANTIGUA PASTELERÍA DEL POZO

Spanish cakes may not be as delicate as French or Austrian pastries, but there are many with a tale to tell. This bakery dates back to 1830 and is known for its *roscones de Reyes*, a sweet bread associated with the Three Kings festival (6 January). But these rings of brioche-style bread, dotted with sugar and glazed fruits, are made on the premises year-round. Alternatively, go for the tarts filled with pumpkin

jam and custard. Closed Sun, mid-Jul to end Aug.
🔲 F7 ✉ Calle Pozo 8 ☎ 91 522 38 94 🔘 Sol

CASA DE DIEGO

www.casadiego.net
This 150-year-old store is still the best place in Madrid to buy a real fan. They range from cheap and cheerful for use on hot days to exquisite hand-painted collector's items. Also umbrellas and walking sticks.
🔲 F9 ✉ Plaza de la Puerta del Sol 12 ☎ 91 522 66 43 🔘 Sol

CASA JIMÉNEZ

www.casajimenez.net
For over 80 years, this family-run store has sold the finest embroidered

WHAT'S ON OFFER?

The little specialist shops of Madrid can offer much insight into the minds of the city's inhabitants. Sometimes the shop's layout is so irrational that it is hard to know what the place is really selling. Particularly in the area around the Plaza Mayor, the district of La Latina and the area between Calle del Barco and Calle Hortaleza, just off the Gran Vía, it is worth pausing to admire off-beat window displays. These have been lovingly put together by proprietors who know they are as much a part of the urban landscape as any monument.

veils and shawls. Some are works of art in their own right, and so are often framed rather than worn.
🔲 E/F7 ✉ Calle de Preciados 42 ☎ 91 548 05 26 🔘 Callao, Santo Domingo

EL CORTE INGLÉS

www.elcorteingles.es
Spain's pride and joy, a department store that sells everything, and ensures good value for money. Some 20 stores in Madrid, including the flagship store on Calle de Preciados, just off the Puerta del Sol.
🔲 F7 ✉ Calle de Preciados 1 ☎ 91 379 80 00 🔘 Sol

LA FAVORITA

The first top hats and bowler hats were sold here on the Plaza Mayor back in 1894. The shop somehow survives on more modern head gear, such as caps (*gorras*) and berets.
🔲 F7 ✉ Plaza Mayor 25 ☎ 91 366 58 77 🔘 Sol

FELIX ANTIGÜEDADES

An antiques shop in the heart of the Rastro flea market where you'll find an intriguing collection of *objets d'art*, especially Oriental art and musical instruments.
🔲 F9 ✉ Plaza General Vara del Rey 3 ☎ 91 528 48 30 🔘 La Latina

EL FLAMENCO VIVE

There is no doubt that flamenco lives inside

Alberto Martínez's shop, Spain's first devoted to flamenco. In addition to a good selection of music, there are books on flamenco history and much flamenco paraphernalia.
🚹 E7 ✉ Calle Conde de Lemos 7 ☎ 91 547 39 17 🔘 Opera

FNAC
Five floors of books and CDs, plus a small concert area. Also has foreign newspapers, photograph developing services and a ticket agency.
🚹 F7 ✉ Calle de Preciados 28 ☎ 91 595 62 00 🔘 Callao

GALERÍAS PIQUÉR
This pleasant mall in the Rastro street market has 20 antiques shops. Try Siglo 20 for art deco, and El Estudio for Isabelline furniture and lamps.
🚹 F9 ✉ Calle Ribera de Curtidores 29 🔘 La Latina

GUITARRAS RAMÍREZ
www.guitarrasramirez.com Since 1882, four generations of the Ramírez family have made and sold some of Spain's finest guitars for classical and flamenco music. Bought by amateurs as well as world-famous professional musicians.
🚹 F7/8 ✉ Calle de la Paz 8 ☎ 91 531 42 29 🔘 Sol

MARIANO MADRUEÑO
The Spanish drink a wide range of their own wines,

as well as unusual liqueurs such as *pacharán* (sloe gin). Barrels and alembics still decorate this century-old *bodega* (wine shop), near the Monasterio de las Descalzas Reales. It's still run by the same family and you will find the staff helpful with what is an eclectic selection.
🚹 F7 ✉ Calle Postigo de San Martín 3 ☎ 91 521 19 55 🔘 Callao

SESEÑA
With a firm eye on maintaining quality control, this family establishment, dating back to 1901, specializes in capes. Pablo Picasso, Michael Jackson, and Hillary Clinton have all been customers.
🚹 F7/8 ✉ Calle de la Cruz 23 ☎ 91 531 68 40 🔘 Sol

SHOPPING AROUND
For better or worse, the retail scene in Madrid is increasingly dominated by chain stores and *centros comerciales* (shopping malls). Try and get into the back streets to visit smaller establishments. Shop assistants can be sloth-like when it comes to serving customers they don't know, and 'service with a smile' is only now starting to catch on. Larger stores are open through lunch, while smaller ones continue to close from about 1.30 to about 4.30.

STAMPS AND COINS MARKET
People meet to discuss stamps and coins under the archways of the Plaza Mayor.
🚹 F7/8 ✉ Plaza Mayor 🕐 Sunday morning 🔘 Sol

LA VIOLETA
This tiny shop could be out of a fairy tale. It specializes in an unusual sweet: real sugared violets in jars and pretty little boxes. It also sells chocolates and candied fruits, and everything is wrapped elegantly to make the ideal present.
🚹 F7 ✉ Plaza de Canalejas 6 ☎ 91 522 55 22 🔘 Sol

VIPS
www.clubvips.com The 12 bright, bold VIPS stores around the city, convenient and impressive in size, sell books, magazines and CDs, along with food and gifts. Most are open 24 hours. Each also has a bar and restaurant.
🚹 F7 ✉ Gran Vía 65 (with branches throughout the city) ☎ 91 547 72 54 🔘 Callao

ZARA
Now a household name around the world, Spanish chain Zara has five main-street stores in Madrid, offering stylish mainstream fashion for men and women at down-to-earth prices.
🚹 F7 ✉ Gran Vía 32 ☎ 91 521 12 83 🔘 Gran Vía

Entertainment and Nightlife

ARCO DE CUCHILLEROS

At this *tablao flamenco*, close to the Plaza Mayor, top flamenco dancers and singers have performed for nearly 50 years. Rather than a theatre or nightclub, this is more a bar with entertainment, so have a drink and watch the action between 9pm and 2am. Closed Monday.

✚ E8 ✉ Calle Cuchilleros 7 ☎ 91 364 02 63 Ⓜ Sol

BERLIN CABARET 1930

www.berlincabaret.com
The Spanish still love magic tricks, as well as the usual risqué song and dance, drag shows and high-kicking chorus lines. Expect lots of red velvet and a happy crowd. But, be warned: shows at this café-theatre often start as late as 1am.

✚ E8 ✉ Costanilla de San Pedro 11 ☎ 91 366 20 34 Ⓜ La Latina, Ópera

LA BOCA DEL LOBO

'The Jaws of the Wolf' is a lively dance bar where the music can be anything from hip-hop to rock 'n' roll, depending on the DJ. Dark, smoky atmosphere. Open from 10pm till late.

✚ G7/8 ✉ Calle Echegaray 11 ☎ 91 429 70 13 Ⓜ Sevilla

THE BOURBON CAFÉ

www.thebourboncafe.net
Choose between the disco and the live bands at this youth-oriented club. The disco has themed nights, from Mexican to hip-hop; live bands range from rock and jazz to Latin and flamenco pop. Out-and-out fun, with lots of loud music and fast food, from hamburgers to pizzas, served till 1am.

✚ F7 ✉ Calle Carrera de San Jerónimo 5 ☎ 91 532 58 57 Ⓜ Sol

CAFÉ CENTRAL

One of the best jazz venues in Europe. There are performances every night, mainly from Spanish, but sometimes foreign, musicians.

✚ F8 ✉ Plaza del Ángel 10 ☎ 91 369 41 43 Ⓒ Daily 10.30pm Ⓜ Sevilla, Antón Martín, Sol

CAFÉ POPULART

Live music every day—jazz, blues and swing—in a comfortable environment with intelligent conversation.

✚ G8 ✉ Calle Huertas 22 ☎ 91 429 84 07 Ⓜ Antón Martín

RAVE ON

The limitless capacity of *madrileños* for having fun has made Madrid a dance club owner's dream. The city is the undisputed European nightlife capital, and the night begins and ends very late indeed.

LAS CARBONERAS

Madrid's newest flamenco club is already rated by *aficionados* for its quality acts. The show begins around 11pm, but arrive earlier if you want to be sure of a seat.

✚ E8 ✉ Calle del Conde de Miranda 1 ☎ 91 542 86 77 Ⓜ Sol

CASA PATAS

The best-known of Madrid's flamenco *tablaos* is a little touristy, but none the less enjoyable. Live midnight performances, more frequent in May.

✚ F8 ✉ Calle Cañizares 10 ☎ 91 369 15 74/04 96 Ⓒ Thu–Sat midnight Ⓜ Tirso de Molina, Antón Martín

CERVECERÍA ALEMANA

One of the city's most popular bars. A good meeting place in the Santa Ana district.

✚ F8 ✉ Plaza de Santa Ana 6 ☎ 91 429 70 33 Ⓜ Antón Martín

CINE DORÉ

A restored old cinema and now the seat of Filmoteca Española, the national film institute, and a mecca for film buffs. Most of the films shown are in their original language with subtitles in Spanish. Even when there's nothing on, it has a good bar-restaurant and bookshop.

✚ G8 ✉ Santa Isabel 3 Ⓜ Antón Martín

CENTRO

ENTERTAINMENT AND NIGHTLIFE

LE COCK

Round off the evening with a cocktail or two beneath the glass roof of this tastefully decorated late-night bar.
🔂 G7 ⊠ Calle Reina 16
☎ 91 532 28 26 🔘 Banco de España

LA COQUETTE

The only Madrid bar dedicated exclusively to blues is very 1960s.
🔂 E/F7 ⊠ Calle de las Hileras 14 🔘 Ópera

LA CORRALA

La Corrala is used for open-air *zarzuela* performances in summer.
🔂 F9 ⊠ Calle Tribulete 12
☎ No phone 🔘 Lavapiés

GLASS BAR

A bar in the lobby of the Hotel Urban, with lots of glass, expensive cocktails and music that ranges from disco and soul to funky and pop.
🔂 G7 ⊠ Carrera de San Jerónimo 34 🔘 Daily 11am–3am ☎ 91 787 77 70
🔘 Sol, Antón Martín

JOY ESLAVA (MADRID)

Plush, though not forbiddingly stylish, club in an 1850s theatre. The central location attracts a diverse clientele.
🔂 F7 ⊠ Calle Arenal 11
☎ 91 366 37 33 🔘 Ópera

PALACIO DE GAVIRIA

One of Madrid's more remarkable night-time locations. An 1851 palace, with fixtures and furniture generally intact, it reopened in 1981 as a nightspot. With its grand staircase entrance and 14 halls, it is well worth checking out.
🔂 F7 ⊠ Calle Arenal 9
☎ 91 526 60 69 🔘 Sol

THE PENTHOUSE LOUNGE AND TERRACE

For spectacular views and equally spectacular cocktails, such as their very own Lavender Margarita, head to the top floor of the hip new ME Madrid Reina Victoria Hotel.
🔂 F8 ⊠ ME Madrid Hotel, Plaza de Santa Ana 14
🔘 Wed–Sat 9pm–4am, Sun 5pm–midnight ☎ 91 701 60 00 🔘 Sol, Antón Martín

TEATRO MONUMENTAL

The place where classical concerts are recorded for broadcast by the Spanish Radio and Televison Orchestra and Choir.

ZARZUELA

In the words of Edmundo de Amici, writing in 1870, the *zarzuela* is 'a piece of music somewhere between comedy and melodrama, between opera and vaudeville, with prose and verse, both recited and sung, serious and lighthearted, a very Spanish and very entertaining musical form.' Among audiences of a certain age, it remains as popular as ever.

🔂 G8 ⊠ Calle Atocha 65
☎ 91 429 12 81 🔘 Antón Martín

TEATRO DE LA ZARZUELA

Light opera called *zarzuela* is particularly popular with the older generation in Madrid. Even if you don't speak Spanish, the farcical plots are so simple that anyone can understand them. And the music and singing are top class. Enjoy it at this glitzy 150-year-old theatre.
🔂 G7 ⊠ Jovellanos 4
☎ 91 524 54 00 🔘 Varies, check schedule 🔘 Antón Martín

TORRES BERMEJAS

www.torresbermejas.com
For over 40 years, this restaurant and club has hosted some of the most famous flamenco singers and dancers in the world. The setting is reminiscent of the Alhambra palace in Granada. Eat traditional Spanish dishes, such as paella, and then enjoy the show. More for tourists than locals.
🔂 F7 ⊠ Mesonero Romanos 11 ☎ 91 532 33 22
🔘 Callao

VIVA MADRID

The tiled *azulejo* frontage of Viva Madrid bar has been photographed for a thousand guide books.
🔂 G8 ⊠ Calle Manuel Fernández y González 7
☎ 91 429 36 40 🔘 Antón Martín

Restaurants

PRICES

Prices are approximate, based on a 3-course meal for one person.

€€€   over €45
€€   €25–€45
€   under €25

BOTÍN (€€)

www.botin.es
Botín first opened its doors in 1725, making it, according to the *Guinness Book of Records*, the world's oldest restaurant. Suckling pig, roasted in a wood-fired oven, is the Castillian speciality dish.

⊞ E8 ⊠ Calle Cuchilleros 17 ☎ 91 366 42 17 ⓜ La Latina

LOS CARACOLES (€)

How authentic do you want? This is all about snails: casseroled, with lots of garlic. Wash them down with a glass of draft vermouth. Eat standing up; feel like a local.

⊞ E9 ⊠ Calle de Toledo 106 ☎ 91 366 42 46 ⓒ Tue–Sat 9am–11pm, Sun till 7.30pm ⓜ Puerta de Toledo

CASA ALBERTO (€€)

www.casaalberto.es
Characterful restaurant, founded in 1827, at the back of a bar that serves terrific tapas. It's full of bullfighting memorabilia. The ham croquettes and oxtail are recommended.

⊞ G8 ⊠ Calle Huertas 18 ☎ 91 429 93 56 ⓒ Closed Sun night, Mon and 2 weeks in Aug ⓜ Antón Martín

CASA LABRA (€–€€)

www.casalabra.com
The Spanish Socialist Party was founded here in 1879, just 19 years after the bar was established, and Casa Labra has been producing typically *madrileño* tapas ever since. Tasty cod croquettes are a house special.

⊞ F7 ⊠ Calle Tetuán 12 ☎ 91 532 14 05 ⓜ Sol

CERVECERÍA CERVANTES (€)

Packed with locals looking for the best fish and seafood tapas in town. Just point at what you fancy. The *tostada de gamba*, hot shrimps in aioli on toast, are quite delicious.

⊞ G8 ⊠ Plaza de Jesús 7 ☎ 91 429 60 93 ⓒ Daily 11am–midnight. Closed Sun evening ⓜ Antón Martín

CHOCOLATERÍA SAN GINÉS (€)

Flashy, big and extremely busy, especially in winter.

NEW TASTES

For historical and geographical reasons, both Latin American and North African cuisines are increasingly popular on Madrid's hitherto fairly conservative culinary scene. The menus can be as incomprehensible to Spaniards as to any visitor. The best bet is to see what others are eating and order what looks appealing.

Three minutes from Sol.

⊞ F7 ⊠ Pasaje de San Ginés 5 ☎ 91 365 65 46 ⓜ Sol, Ópera

ERROTA-ZAR (€€)

www.errota-zar.com
Opposite the Teatro de la Zarzuela, this has been one of the city's most authentic Basque restaurants for over 20 years. Specialities include fried fresh anchovies, tartare of bonito and a variety of traditional dishes using hake, string beans or mushrooms. As well as local cheeses, there are good desserts, such as chocolate cake and ice cream. The wine cellar has over 10,000 bottles.

⊞ G7 ⊠ Calle Jovellanos 3 (first floor) ☎ 91 531 25 64 ⓒ Daily; closed Sun ⓜ Banco de España

LA ESQUINA DEL CAFÉ (€)

Tiny corner café that is known for its yummy desserts, such as tiramisu and chocolate cake. Ideal for a break from tapas, with a *café con leche* (coffee with hot milk).

⊞ G8 ⊠ Calle de Jesús 10 ☎ 91 369 30 84 ⓒ Mon–Thu 12.30–5, Fri, Sat 12.30pm–2am, Sun 12.30–6 ⓜ Antón Martín

LHARDY (€€–€€€)

www.lhardy.com
One of the city's classier restaurants and a local institution. The good range of fairly pricey tapas downstairs includes consommé, croquettes,

Russian salad on bread and, in summer, Madrid's best gazpacho. There is also a delicatessen.

🚹 F7 ⊠ Calle Carrera de San Jerónimo 8 ☎ 91 521 33 85 ⏺ Closed dinner, Sun, public hols 🚇 Sol

POSADA DE LA VILLA (€€€)

www.posadadelavilla.com
The building just off the Plaza Mayor dates back to 1642 and the atmosphere and dishes are about as traditional as you can get. This is the place to order Madrid oven-roast lamb and cocido (Madrid's favourite stew; order 24 hours in advance). Locals are as happy here as tourists.

🚹 E8 ⊠ Cava Baja 9 ☎ 91 366 18 60 ⏺ Closed Sun dinner 🚇 Latina, Tirso de Molina, Sol

RESTAURANTE MOAÑA (€€€)

In an old-fashioned and rather formal setting, chef Francisco Romero Vieitez reworks traditional Galician recipes for fish and seafood. Choose from scallops, lobster, cod and more. Wide range of Galician wines.

🚹 E7 ⊠ Calle de las Hileras 4 ☎ 91 548 29 14 ⏺ Closed Sun, dinner 🚇 Ópera

TABERNA DE ANTONIO SÁNCHEZ (€)

The best-conserved of all the tapas bars pays homage to the bullfighting family that has run it since 1830. Displays on bullfighting make the distinctive setting as fascinating as the tapas.

🚹 F8 ⊠ Calle Mesón de Paredes 13 ☎ 91 539 78 26 🚇 Tirso de Molina

TABERNA MACEIRA (€)

Join the madrileños standing outside and wait for a table in this popular Galician-style haunt. Menus are on artists' palettes, the music is Galician bagpipes and the helpings are large: pulpo (octopus), patatas bravas (spicy potatoes) and jugs of sangría. Cramped, noisy, good value and good fun. Cash only, no reservations.

🚹 G8 ⊠ Calle de las Huertas 66 ☎ 91 429 58 18 ⏺ Daily 1–4.30, 10.30–1 🚇 Antón Martín

---

MADRID GASTRONOMY

Madrid and its region have a distinctive style of cooking, which is plain, straightforward and tasty. Asado means roast, and there's nothing better than roast lamb or kid from a wood-fired oven. The other major local favourite is cocido, a stew with meat, chick peas and vegetables. These are cooked together in a clay pot, right in the fireplace. Match these with the regional red wines made from Tempranillo grapes.

LA TAURINA (€)

This is a shrine to bullfighting, with everything from bulls' heads and capes to sequined matador costumes and tiled murals of bullfights. But it is also a great place for tapas and heartier home-cooked Andalucian dishes, such as oxtail, gazpacho, black pudding, squid, tortilla and anchovies.

🚹 F7 ⊠ Carrera de San Jerónimo 5 ☎ 91 531 39 69 ⏺ Daily 🚇 Sol

VINOTECA BARBECHERA (€)

www.vinoteca-barbechera.com
Part of a successful chain of wine bars, this is a good place to see modern Madrid at play. Good range of snacks: platters of smoked tuna and trout, rolls stuffed with chorizo, ham or anchovies, crêpes for dessert, plus a wide range of wines by the glass from Spain and abroad. Six venues in Madrid, including one in Chueca.

🚹 G8 ⊠ Calle del Príncipe 27 ☎ 91 420 04 78 ⏺ Daily 10am–midnight 🚇 Antón Martín, Sol

VIUDA DE VACAS (€)

Madrileños like to bring overseas visitors here for traditional Spanish cooking amid azulejo tiles and wooden tables.

🚹 E8 ⊠ Calle Cava Alta 23 ☎ 91 366 58 47 ⏺ Closed Sun night 🚇 La Latina

With one of the world's most famous art museums and one of the world's great urban parks, this part of Madrid is a magnet for visitors. But don't miss the Real Fábrica de Tapices, the tapestry factory, where tradition rules.

Sights	70–77	Top 25	
Shopping	78	Museo del Prado ▷ 70	
		Parque del Retiro ▷ 73	
Entertainment		Plaza de la Cibeles ▷ 74	
and Nightlife	79	Puerto de Alcalá ▷ 75	
Restaurants	79–80		

TOP
25

Jerónimos and the East

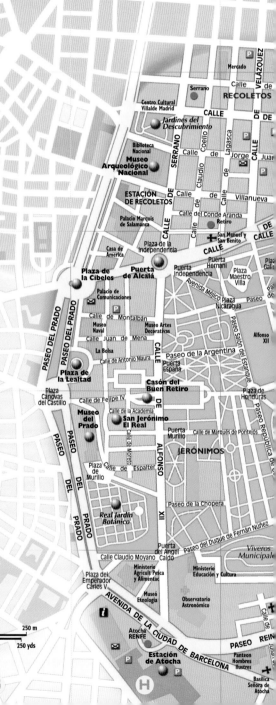

5

Mercado

Calle
RECOLETOS
Serrano

Centro Cultural
Villa de Madrid

Jardines del
Descubrimiento

Coello

CALLE

DE

DE

de

Lagasca

6

Biblioteca
Nacional

**Museo
Arqueológico
Nacional**

SERRANO

Calle

de

Jorge

Juan

Claudio

de

CALLE

**ESTACIÓN
DE RECOLETOS**

Calle

de

Villanueva

DE

Palacio Marquís
de Salamanca

Calle del Conde Aranda
Retiro

Casa de
América

Plaza de la
Independencia

CALLE

San Manuel y
San Benito

DE

CALLE

**Plaza de
la Cibeles**

**Puerta
de Alcalá**

Puerta
Independencia

Puerta
Hernani

Plaza
Galdó

Palacio de
Comunicaciones

Avenida Mélico

Plaza
Maestro
Villa

7

Calle de Montalbán

Museo
Naval

Museo Artes
Decorativas

Plaza
Nicaragua

Paseo

Pa

Alfonso
XII

PASEO DEL PRADO

PASEO DEL PRADO

Calle Juan de Mena

La Bolsa

Paseo de la Argentina

Calle de Antonio Maura

Puerta
España

Paseo Salón del Estanque

**Plaza de
la Lealtad**

**Casón del
Buen Retiro**

Plaza
Canovas
del Castillo

Calle de Felipe IV

DE

Plaza de
Honduras

**Museo
del Prado**

Calle de la Academia

**San Jerónimo
El Real**

ALFONSO

Puerta
Murillo

Calle de Marqués de Pontejos

Paseo República de C

8

PASEO

PASEO

Calle de Morutti

JERÓNIMOS

Plaza
de
Murillo

Calle de Espalter

DEL

DEL

Paseo de la Chopera

PRADO

PRADO

XII

**Real Jardín
Botánico**

Puerta
del Angel
Caido

Paseo del Duque de Fernán Núñez

Viveros
Municipale

Calle Claudio Moyano

Caido

Plaza del
Emperador
Cárlos V

Ministerio
Agricult Pesca
y Alimentac

Ministerio
Educación y Cultura

Museó
Etnologia

Observatorio
Astronómico

Calle de

9

AVENIDA DE LA CIUDAD DE BARCELONA

0   250 m

0   250 yds

ℹ️

Atocha
RENFE

PASEO

REIN

Panteón
Hombres
Ilustres

**Estación
de Atocha**

Ⓗ

Basilica
Señora de
Atocha

G

SALAMANCA

Hermosilla

Velázquez

GOYA

La Concepción

Archivo Heráldico

ALCALÁ

O'DONNELL

DE

Puerta de Madrid

Plaza Costa Rica

Glorieta Sevilla

Bolivia

Colombia

Plaza de Guatemala

Glorieta Sardana

Paseo de Venezuela

Jardines del Arquit Herrero Palacios

Palacio de Velázquez

Palacio de Cristal

Parque del Retiro

Jardines de Cecilio Rodriguez

Hospital del Niño Jesús

Puerta Granada

Glorieta del Angel Caido

Paseo Uruguay

La Rosaleda

Puerta del Pacífico

Calle Poeta Esteban Villegas

Calle Andrés

CRISTINA

Torrelón

Plaza Mariano de Cavia

PACÍFICO

Real Fábrica de Tapices

Calle de Castelló

PRÍNCIPE DE VERGARA

CALLE

Príncipe de Vergara

Calle del General Pardiñas

Calle Antonio Acuña

AVENIDA

DE

MENÉNDEZ

Paseo del Duque de Fernán Núñez

PELAYO

Paseo del Duque de Fernán Núñez

MENÉNDEZ Y PELAYO

Calle de Reyes Magos

Calle de Gutenberg

AVENIDA

J

K

L

Jerónimos and the East

Museo del Prado

HIGHLIGHTS

● *Las Meninas*, Velázquez
● Goya's 'dark paintings'
● *The 2nd of May, The 3rd of May, Las Majas*, Goya
● *The Holy Family*, Raphael
● *The Bacchanal, Emperor Charles V in Mühlberg*, Titian
● *The Garden of Earthly Delights*, Bosch
● *The Triumph of Death*, Brueghel
● *Self Portrait*, Dürer
● *David and Goliath*, Caravaggio
● *The Three Graces*, Rubens

TIPS

● Weekends are always crowded; plan to go first thing in the morning, or at the end of the day.
● When renovated, the Casón del Buen Retiro will house the Prado's collection of 19th-century art.

The city's pride in the magnificent Prado is justified. With its Goyas, El Grecos and other masterpieces, it is undoubtedly one of the great art museums of the world.

Brief history The neoclassical building, completed by Juan de Villanueva in 1785, was conceived by Charles III as a centre for the study of natural sciences. After Napoléon's troops damaged it during the Spanish Wars of Succession, it was restored by Fernando VII as a home for the royal collection of paintings and sculptures and opened as a museum in November 1819. It is unequalled in the world, with a collection numbering 7,000 pictures, of which around 1,500 are on display at any given time; there are 115 Goyas, 83 works by Rubens, 50 by Velázquez, 40 Brueghels, 36 Titians, 32 El Grecos and 20 Zurbaráns. With the

The Museo del Prado has over 1,500 paintings on diplay, but don't miss those by Goya, Velázquez, El Greco, Brueghel and Titian

opening of the extension in 2007, the museum gained much-needed space for temporary exhibitions. Like all great museums, the Prado is best appreciated in more than one visit.

Velázquez and Goya Do not leave the Prado without seeing Velázquez's masterpiece, *Las Meninas*, widely considered technically the finest painting in the world. Goya's *Majas*—two paintings believed to be of the Duchess of Alba, one naked, one clothed—positively beckon the spectator into the picture, Madrid's seductive answer to the Mona Lisa. Goya's *pinturas negras*—among them *Saturn Devouring One of his Sons* and *Half-Drowned Dog*—are obviously the work of a man whose sanity is in decline. At once grotesque, disturbing and breathtaking, they are unique.

THE BASICS

www.museoprado.es

🚼 H8

✉ Paseo del Prado

🕐 Tue–Sun 9–8, public hols 9–2

☎ 91 330 28 00

🍴 Restaurant, café

Ⓜ Banco de España, Atocha

🚌 9, 10, 14, 19, 27, 34, 37, 45

🚊 Atocha, Recoletos

♿ Moderate. Free to under 18s, over 65s; Tue–Sat 6pm–8pm, Sun 5pm–8pm

Monument to Alfonso XII (opposite and right); fun in the park (left)

Parque del Retiro

Small enough to be welcoming, but large enough to get pleasantly lost in, the Retiro will linger in your memory, particularly if you see it in late spring or early autumn, when its colours are most vivid.

History On a sunny Sunday afternoon, the whole city seems drawn to the Retiro park, 1.2sq km (0.5sq miles) in the city centre, whose name translates as 'retreat'. Originally thickly wooded and once a hunting ground for Philip II, the Retiro was the brainchild of the Duke of Olivares, who designed it in the 1630s for Philip IV as part of the Buen Retiro Palace—a complex of royal buildings and immense formal gardens that inspired Louis XIV at Versailles. It was used until the time of Charles III, who partially opened it to the public in the 1770s. Most of the palace was destroyed during the Napoleonic Wars.

A walk in the park Use the entrance on Calle Alfonso XII, opposite the Casón del Buen Retiro. Walk through the parterre gardens and up the steps along a broad, shady avenue to the lake. If you want to take a boat out, head left around the lake; opposite you is a statue of Alfonso XII, a popular spot to soak up the sun. Otherwise, turn right and follow the Paseo de Republica de Cuba. From here, you can take one of many paths leading to the Palacio de Cristál (Glass Palace), the Retiro's loveliest building. Constructed in 1886, it is one of several exhibition spaces within the park. At the southern end of the park is La Rosaleda (the Rose Garden), in full glory in May.

THE BASICS

🔲 H7–J8
✉ Calle Alcalá, Alfonso XII, Avenida de Menedez Pelayo, Paseo de la Reina Cristina
🕐 May–Sep 6am–midnight; Oct–Apr 6am–10pm
🍴 Terrazas
🚇 Retiro, Atocha, Ibiza
🚌 2, 14, 19, 20, 26, 28
🚉 Atocha, Retiro

HIGHLIGHTS

● Palacio de Cristál
● Artichoke Fountain in the Rose Garden
● Cecilio Rodríguez Gardens
● Velázquez Palace
● Statue of Alfonso XII
● Lake
● Fallen Angel statue
● 400-year-old cypress tree near Philip IV entrance
● Philip IV parterre
● Observatory (1790)
● Free band concerts from May to October
● Puppet shows for children on Sunday

Plaza de la Cibeles

The fountain of La Cibeles, on Plaza de la Cibeles (left and right)

THE BASICS

+ H7
⊠ Plaza de la Cibeles
🚇 Banco de España
🚌 5, 9, 10, 14, 20, 27, 34, 45, 51, 53 and all night buses
🚉 Atocha, Recoletos

HIGHLIGHTS

● Post Office
● Gardens of Palacio de Linares
● Façade of Bank of Spain building
● Robert Michel's lions
● Newspaper stand on Paseo del Prado

Despite the constant traffic, this plaza, a sheer mass of stone around a dramatic statue of the fertility goddess, La Cibeles, is Madrid's most overwhelming square.

Cars pass by Seated imperiously at one of Madrid's busiest intersections, the goddess and her marble fountain were erected according to instructions from Charles III (1716–88). The main statue is by Francisco Gutiérrez and the lions, Hipponomes and Atlanta, drawing the goddess' chariot, are by Robert Michel. Originally at the corner of the square, the statue was finally completed in 1792 and moved in 1895, at which date the cherubim were added.

Around the plaza The enormous wedding-cake look-alike on the southeastern side of the square is one of Madrid's most imposing buildings. It was designed by Antonio Palacios in 1904, its painstakingly worked façade reminiscent of Viennese style. Designed by Antonio Palacios in 1904 to be the Palacio de Comunicaciones (Central Post Office), it was dubbed by local wits as Our Lady of Communications, as if it were a cathedral. The building is now used by the Madrid City Council.

The Palacio de Linares The real treasure of the Plaza de la Cibeles is the elaborately decorated Palacio de Linares. It was designed in 1872, and restored and opened in 1992 as the Casa de América. It now showcases exhibits about Latin American visual arts.

The five-arched Puerta de Alcalá is a symbol of Madrid

Puerta de Alcalá

If you are travelling from the airport by taxi to Madrid's centre, this gateway is one of the first things you will see. It is perhaps the city's most powerful emblem, particularly when lit at night.

Neoclassical symbol Listed as a National Monument, the Puerta de Alcalá, in the Plaza de la Independencia, is one of the great symbols of Madrid. It is perhaps the city's finest example of the neoclassical architecture that came as a reaction to previous baroque excesses. Commissioned by Charles III, who was to be responsible for so much of the city's architectural transformation, it was designed by Francisco Sabatini in 1778 as the main entrance to the Court. Best appreciated when floodlit at night, the Puerta de Alcalá stands in the middle of an immense traffic junction, so it can be admired only from a distance.

Design Made up of five arches of granite and stone, the statue has 10 columns similar to those by Michelangelo for the Capitol in Rome—facing east and crowned with Ionic capitals. Three central archways are flanked by two smaller ones. The lion heads in the middle of the three higher arches are the work of Robert Michel, and the cherubim, the trophies and the coat of arms that surmount the statue are by Francisco Gutiérrez. You can still see the bullet marks from the 1921 assassination attempt on Eduardo Dato, President of Madrid's Council of Ministers, on the north side of the statue. Luckily, a Madrid Town Council proposal to paint parts of the *puerta* white was rejected.

THE BASICS

✚ H7
✉ Plaza de la Independencia
🚇 Retiro
🚌 9, 15, 20, 28, 51, 52
🚏 Recoletos

HIGHLIGHTS

● Views of the monument when lit at night
● The lion heads designed by Robert Michel
● Bullet holes from a 1921 assassination attempt

More to See

CASÓN DEL BUEN RETIRO

www.museoprado.es

This was originally the ballroom of the Buen Retiro Royal Palace, a building destroyed by Napoleonic troops but rebuilt by Charles III, who had the vault decorated with frescoes. It holds free temporary exhibitions.

H8 ✉ Calle Alfonso XII 68 ☎ 902 10 70 77 🚇 Retiro, Banco de España 🚌 19

ESTACIÓN DE ATOCHA

Some 2,000sq m (21,530sq ft) of indoor tropical garden can be found inside this impressive late 19th-century wrought-iron station canopy by Alberto del Palacio. The cylindrical glass tower next to the station is a monument to the 191 victims of the 11 March, 2004 bomb attacks on Madrid trains.

H9 ✉ Plaza del Emperador Carlos V ☎ 902 24 02 02 🚇 Atocha 🚌 14, 27, 34, 37, 45 ♿ Few

JARDINES DEL DESCUBRIMIENTO

Typical of Madrid town planning of the 1970s, these sculpture gardens in the Plaza de Colón were built to celebrate Spain's role in the discovery of the New World. The gardens are dominated by an 1892 Jerónimo Suñol statue of Christopher Columbus, but it is the wonderful Joaquín Vaquero Turcios sculptures from 1977 that are the real highlight. Underneath the gardens is the Centro Cultural de la Villa de Madrid.

H6 ✉ Plaza de Colón 🚇 Recoletos 🚌 1, 5, 9, 14, 19, 21, 27, 37, 45, 51, 53, 74, 89

MUSEO ARQUEOLÓGICO NACIONAL

Spain's national archaeological museum is closed for major refurbishment but a 'best of' selection from the collection, including many fabulous finds from Prehistoric times and the Middle Ages, is open in the meantime.

H6 ✉ Calle de Serrano 🚇 Serrano, Retiro 🚌 1, 9, 19, 51, 74

PLAZA DE LA LEALTAD

A stone's throw from the Prado, this elegant, semicircular plaza dominated by the Ritz Hotel has an obelisk in the

Estación de Atocha

Casón del Buen Retiro

middle to the memory of those who died at the hands of Napoleonic troops on 3 May 1808. Their ashes are kept in an urn at the base of the monument. The Madrid Stock Exchange was built here in 1884, in a neoclassical design that neatly echoes the Prado.

➕ H7 ✉ Plaza de la Lealtad 🚇 Banco de España 🚌 10, 14, 27, 34, 37, 45

REAL FÁBRICA DE TAPICES

www.realfabricadetapices.com

The centuries-old craft of creating tapestries and carpets continues in the Royal Tapestry Factory. The looms still hum as they did back in the 18th century, when the Flemish van der Goten family founded the works. On the tour (about 40 minutes) you learn that many of the original designs were created by Goya and other famous artists, and that it can take four months to finish one square metre.

➕ J9 ✉ Calle de Fuenterrabía 2 ☎ 91 434 05 50 🕐 Mon–Fri 10–2. Closed Sat, Sun, Holy Week, Aug 🚇 Atocha, Menéndez Pelayo 🚌 14, 24, 26, 32, 37, 54, 141

🖐 Inexpensive ♿ None

REAL JARDÍN BOTÁNICO

www.rjb.csic.es

These peaceful gardens are the result of overseas expeditions in search of interesting species dating back to the 18th century. The plants and trees are carefully classified and laid out along geometrical walkways. It's the perfect retreat from the city.

➕ H8 ✉ Plaza de Murillo 2 🕐 Daily from 10am; closing varies with season 🚇 Atocha 🚌 10, 14, 27, 34, 37, 45

🖐 Inexpensive

SAN JERÓNIMO EL REAL

Iglesia de San Jerónimo el Real, Madrid's society church, wedged at the side of the Prado, was built back in 1505, but over the centuries renovations included several controversial neo-Gothic additions. The steps at the entrance on Calle Alarcón, for example, were built especially for the wedding of Alfonso XIII and his queen, Victoria Eugenia, in 1906.

➕ H8 ✉ Calle Moreto 4 ☎ 91 420 30 78 🕐 Daily 10–1, 5–8 🚇 Atocha, Banco de España 🚌 Free ♿ Difficult

Craftspeople at work in the Royal Tapestry Factory

Shopping

CORONEL TAPIOCCA

www.coroneltapiocca.com
A chain aimed at the modern-day adventurer, selling everything from rucksacks, trousers and fishing gear to camping and hunting equipment, plus useful things, such as torches. Designed for comfort, the clothes also appeal to the urban dweller who wants to look sporty.

➕ H9 ✉ Glorieta del Emperador Carlos V ☎ 91 467 29 74 Ⓜ Atocha

FABENDI

Established for over 30 years, this is a shop that locals head for when they want something—anything—in leather: leather and suede coats, jackets, trousers and suits. A wide choice.

➕ K9 ✉ Avenida del Mediterráneo 5 ☎ 91 552 24 14 Ⓜ Menéndez Pelayo

GALERÍA DE ARTE VICTORIA HIDALGO

www.victoriahidalgo.com
A step away from the Prado museum. Ever since 1998, this gallery has shown paintings and sculptures by living artists.

➕ H8 ✉ Calle de Ruiz de Alarcón 27 ☎ 91 429 56 65 Ⓜ Banco de España

IMAGINARIUM

www.imaginarium.es
Much more than a children's toy shop, this is all about what the name promises: imagination. From musical toys to dolls,

the idea is to encourage children to have fun, in a creative, yet educational way. Think inflatable city—with skyscrapers.

➕ H9 ✉ Plaza del Emperador Carlos V ☎ 91 506 21 23 Ⓜ Atocha

EL JARDÍN DE SERRANO

Select shopping mall in two restored 19th-century mansions on the corner of *calles* Goya and Serrano. The well-heeled stores inside sell fashion, jewellery, gifts, toys and accessories.

➕ H6 ✉ Calle de Goya 6–8 ☎ 91 577 00 12 Ⓜ Serrano

MUSEO DEL PRADO

The museum's excellent Palacios y Museos shop is a great place to find quality souvenirs. As well as fine reproductions of famous works, there are silk scarves and blouses, pictures and chocolates, ties and jewellery.

➕ H8 ✉ Paseo del Prado

WHERE TO GO

Madrid's amazing array of antique shops are in three main areas: the *barrio* Salamanca, around the Calle del Prado and Santa Ana, and around the Rastro, particularly down the Calle Ribera de Curtidores–the most likely source for bargains. Many shops do not specialize in any particular goods, but sell a broad selection of merchandise.

☎ 91 330 28 00 Ⓜ Banco de España

NATURA SELECTION

www.naturaselection.es
Dedicated to arts and crafts, plus clothes from South America, Asia and Africa. All are one of a kind, with scarves and bags, lamps and gloves—all made of natural materials such as cotton, silk and leather.

➕ H9 ✉ Plaza del Emperador Carlos V ☎ 91 467 21 28 Ⓜ Atocha

PERFUMERÍA ALVAREZ GOMEZ

www.alvarezgomez.com
There are branches of this long-established perfumery all over Madrid. They sell a huge range of cosmetics and scents, but mostly their own delicate, flowery fragrances and colognes, beautifully bottled and excellent value.

➕ H6 ✉ Calle de Serrano 14 ☎ 91 431 16 56 Ⓜ Retiro

PIEL DE TORO

www.pieldetoro.com
Famous for must-have T-shirts, with a design that looks like a bull, and also like the outline of Spain. Bought by surfers as well as non-sporty fashionistas. Almost directly opposite the Jardín Botánico. This is a trendy Madrid souvenir shop for adults as well as children.

➕ H8 ✉ Paseo del Prado 42 ☎ 91 360 07 52 Ⓜ Atocha

Entertainment and Nightlife

DISCOTECA AZÚCAR

Even if you cannot dance the salsa, you can have lessons every night at this popular Latin American club where the music is persistent and the crowd is fun, with many clubbers from South America. ➕ J9 ✉ Paseo Reina Cristina 7 ☎ 91 501 61 07 🕒 Daily 11pm–5.30am, Fri, Sat 11.30pm–6.30am Ⓜ Atocha

FLORIDA PARK

www.floridapark.net
Just inside the gates on the eastern side of the Retiro Park, Florida Park has long been a popular destination for out-of-town visitors. With a restaurant, dance floor and stage, this suits those who enjoy a show and dancing late into the night. ➕ J7 ✉ Avenida de Menéndez Pelayo (at Ibiza) ☎ 91 573 78 04 🕒 Daily 9pm–3am. Closed Sun, Mon Ⓜ Ibiza

KAPITAL

www.grupo-kapital.com
With seven floors of dancing, this could be the

MADRID BY NIGHT

With almost 4,000 places to have a drink, Madrid can claim to be Europe's finest city for sheer variety of late-night options—sometimes very late indeed. Main bar areas in the centre are the start of the Paseo de la Castellana (sophisticated), Malasaña (thoroughly unso-phisticated), La Latina and Santa Ana (somewhere in between), and Chueca (gay).

---

biggest club in Madrid. There is everything from salsa, house and karaoke to R'n'B, go-go dancers and a cinema. The great attraction in summer is the rooftop terrace. Although teenagers dominate in the early evening, grown-ups flood in later on, when the dress code is smart-casual. ➕ H9 ✉ Calle de Atocha 125 ☎ 91 420 29 06 🕒 Fri, Sat 5.30pm–10.30pm, Thu–Sun midnight–6am Ⓜ Atocha

EL RETIRO

Sundays in the park (▷ 73) are famous for the entertainers and musicians who keep old and young amused. Outstanding are the summer concerts, called *Veranos de la Villa*.

Restaurants

PRICES

Prices are approximate, based on a 3-course meal for one person.
€€€   over €45
€€   €25–€45
€   under €25

BALZAC (€€€)

www.restaurantebalzac.net
Close to the Prado, this is a special occasion restaurant where service comes with gleaming silverware.

Once known for its Basque cuisine, the menu is now more modern-Mediterranean and sometimes rather daring: pigeon with fruit compote, foie gras salad, pears poached in port. Exceptional wine cellar. ➕ H8 ✉ Calle de Moreto 7 ☎ 91 420 06 13 🕒 Closed Sat lunch, Sun Ⓜ Retiro

LA CASTELA (€€)

A local favourite, this typical *taberna* is part

tapas bar for Spanish snacks, part dining room specializing in Spanish cuisine. ➕ K7 ✉ Calle del Doctor Castelo 22 ☎ 91 574 00 15 🕒 Daily 2–4, 9–midnight. Closed Sun, Aug Ⓜ Ibiza, Príncipe de Vergara

LA GAMELLA (€€€)

www.lagamella.com
On the first floor of a splendid old building that was the birthplace of Spanish philosopher José

Ortega y Gasset, this small American-owned restaurant is across from the Retiro. Here 'fusion' cooking mixes Spanish and American at the top end of the range: steak tartare with a shot of Jack Daniels, a classic Caesar salad and proper burgers.
🔁 H7 ✉ Calle de Alfonso XII 4 ☎ 91 532 45 09
🕐 Daily 1.30pm–4, 9–late. Closed Sat lunch, Sun
🚇 Retiro

LA HOJA (€)
www.lahoja.es
Free-range chicken is the base of all the cooking at this straightforward, family-run restaurant, where the emphasis is on Asturian-style recipes. Not one for vegetarians.
🔁 K7 ✉ Calle del Doctor Castelo 48 ☎ 91 409 25 22
🕐 Daily 1pm–midnight. Closed Sun, Mon dinner
🚇 Ibiza, Príncipe de Vergara

INDICE RESTAURANT AT AC PALACIO DEL RETIRO (€€€)
www.ac-hotels.com
Chef David Herranz takes hotel dining to a new level in this smart, contemporary setting. This chef is known for his delicate touch, and for giving a modern twist to traditional Mediterranean dishes. Topped by an outstanding wine list.
🔁 H7 ✉ Ac Palacio del Retiro Hotel, Calle de Alfonso XII 14 ☎ 91 523 74 60
🕐 Daily lunch, dinner
🚇 Retiro, Banco de España

RESTAURANTE VIRIDIANA (€€€)
www.restauranteviridiana.com
At one of Madrid's finest restaurants, Abraham García is known as a character, but he is also a very fine cook, preparing complex modern dishes using traditional and high-quality Spanish produce. The wine list is one of the best in the city.
🔁 H7 ✉ Calle de Juan de Mena 14 ☎ 91 531 10 39
🕐 Daily 1.30–4, 8.30–midnight 🚇 Banco de España, Retiro

RITZ HOTEL (€€)
www.ritzmadrid.com
What could be more traditional than tea at the Ritz? In the Lobby Bar,

---

TAPAS

The tapa, a snack to accompany your drink, is a part of Spanish culture. It started in the 18th century when Carlos III insisted that his entourage cover their wine with a plate of food to keep dust from getting into it (tapa means 'lid'). Many bars no longer display their wares, which can make it hard to order; it's easier when the tapas are kept behind glass so you can see them before buying. Pay before leaving, rather than on a round-by-round basis. Many cervecerías (late-night bars) sell tapas and make an atmospheric venue for a night-time snack.

---

listen to the pianist, harpist or classical Spanish guitarist as you sip tea and nibble elegant sandwiches, pastries and scones. In summer, the experience is even nicer—take a white wicker chair in the garden for lunch, tapas or dinner.
🔁 H7 ✉ Plaza de la Lealtad 5 ☎ 91 701 67 67 🕐 Daily 4.30–7pm 🚇 Banco de España

SULA (€€–€€€)
www.sula.es
Star chef Quique Dacosta's ultra-cool geometric bar, restaurant and luxury gourmet food shop is geared to leading-edge fashion food. Every dish—from imaginative salads, carpaccios and the finest Spanish hams to pastas and desserts—is a treat for the eye. The wine cellar is one of the city's best.
🔁 J6 ✉ Calle de Jorge Juan 33 ☎ 91 781 61 97 🕐 Daily 12–12 🚇 Velázquez, Retiro

TRATTORIA SANT'ARCANGELO (€€)
www.trattoriasantarcangelo.com
In a semi-basement, just a few steps from the Prado and the Jardín Botánico, this is rated as one of Madrid's best, as well as most authentic, Italian restaurants. Carefully prepared dishes include crispy pizzas, spaghetti with a rich seafood sauce and tiramisu.
🔁 H8 ✉ Calle de Moreto 15 ☎ 91 369 10 93 🕐 Daily 🚇 Banco de España

Although it is known as the city's gay area, Chueca is open to all, with a variety of fun restaurants. Then there is Malasaña; considered clubland by many youngsters, this area is being gentrified.

Sights	84–90	Top 25	**25**
Walk	91	Museo Lázaro Galdiano ▷ 84	
Shopping	92	Museo Sorolla ▷ 86	
Entertainment and Nightlife	93		
Restaurants	94		

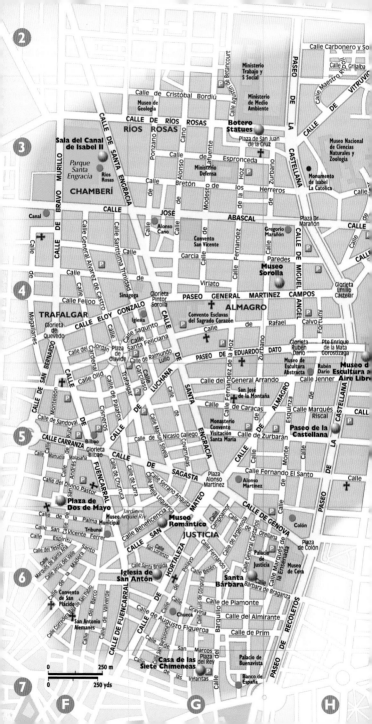

Plaza de la República Argentina

EL VISO

República Argentina

Plaza de la República Argentina

Calle Ballarza

Calle Marqués de Valdeiglesia

Auditorio Nacional de Música

Museo de la Ciudad

Calle de Cartagena

Calle Rafael Rodríguez Marín

Calle Felipe

Calle de Gabriel Lobo

Calle de Cabrera

General Zabala

Calle de Cartagena

CALLE DE JOAQUÍN COSTA

Calle de Campos

Espíritu Santo

Calle Pablo Aranda

Calle Miguel de

Calle San Julio

Calle Antonio Pérez

VELAZQUEZ

PRÍNCIPE DE VERGARA

Cruz del Rayo

Calle de D. Luis

Archivo Histórico Nacional

Calle Castellón de la plana

Calle de

HOYOS

Miguel de los Santos

Calle de D. Quintiliano

Calle de

CALLE DE

Calle Pirilla del Valle

CALLES DE CARTAGENA

Glorieta López de Hoyos

de Pedro de

Valdivia

Calle San Fernando de Jarama

Avenida de América

P

AVENIDA DE AMÉRICA

Gimnasio Moscardó

MARÍA DE LOPEZ DE MOLINA

Avenida de América

FRANCISCO SILVELA

P

Calle de Coslada

Museo Lázaro Galdiano

VELAZQUEZ

Balboa

Castelló

DE VERGARA

Calle Coello

Lagasca

del

General

Santa Mónica

Oráa

Calle

Convento P Dominicos

CALLE

DIEGO

de

de

DE

Pardiñas

Diego de León

Porlier

SERRANO

San Francisco de Borja

La Virgen Peregrino

DE

PRÍNCIPE

LEÓN

General

Calle

de

Núñez de Balboa

Maldonado

Calle de Maldonado

Díaz

Museo de Arte Infantil

CALLE DE JUAN BRAVO

Núñez

CALLE DE JUAN BRAVO

CASTELLANA

Calle

P

de

Padilla

CALLE

Ntra Sra del Pilar

Calle

San Andrés Flamencos

Fundación Juan March

Calle de Padilla

P

JOSÉ

ORTEGA Y GASSET

Castelló

Plaza Marqués de Salamanca

CALLE JOSÉ ORTEGA Y GASSET

DE

Coello

Lagasca

Don Ramón de

Balboa

Cruz

Rosario

Núñez de Balboa

Calle

de

Núñez

Santa M␣ de Monte Carmelo

PRÍNCIPE DE VERGARA

de

Calle de Ayala

P

Calle de Claudio

Calle

Calle

Ayala

de

J

K

Chueca and the North

Museo Lázaro Galdiano

HIGHLIGHTS

● *Landscape*, Gainsborough
● *St. John in Patmos*, Bosch
● *Luis de Góngora*, Velázquez
● *The Adoration of the Magi*, El Greco

TIP

● Take one of the free guided tours on Sat or Sun at 11.30.

There cannot be many museums like this wonderful oddity, which is surprisingly unfamiliar to many *madrileños*. Every time you go there is something new to discover in this dazzling collection.

A noble art collector   José Lázaro Galdiano, an obsessive, seemingly unfocused art collector who died in 1948 at the age of 80, was born into Navarre nobility. He married Paola Florido, an Argentinian who shared his affinity for art, and together they devoted their lives to travelling the world in search of treasures. An essentially private man, Galdiano never revealed how much he paid for any of the masterpieces. On his death, he donated his collection to the state, and the museum opened in 1951. Now completely reorganized, the exhibition begins on the ground

Portrait of a Lady *by Thomas Gainsborough* (left); The Crusaders before Jerusalem *by Velázquez (right)*

floor with an assessment of Lázaro's role as patron and collector and displays a representative sample of the collection, which includes paintings by Hieronymus Bosch, Bartolomé Murillo, Rembrandt, Francisco Zurbarán, El Greco, Velázquez, José de Ribera, Turner and Goya, as well as exquisite gold and silverwork, enamelwork, bronzes, medieval stained glass, jewellery, fans and weaponry.

Parque Florido The collection is housed in the Parque Florido, a neo-Renaissance *palazzo* named after Lázaro's wife. The beautifully restored interiors provide a magnificent setting for the treasures on display. Don't miss the spectacular painted ceilings, commissioned specially by Lázaro to decorate what were orginally the family's private apartments. This is the finest of Madrid's smaller art galleries.

THE BASICS

www.flg.es

➕ J4

✉ Serrano 122

☎ 91 561 60 84

🕐 Wed–Mon 10–4.30

🚇 Nuñez de Balboa/ Rubén Dario, Gregorio Marañón

🚌 9, 12, 16, 19, 51

💶 Moderate, free Sun for EU citizens

♿ Good

Museo Sorolla

HIGHLIGHTS

- *La Bata Rosa* (Room II)
- *Self Portrait* (Room III)
- *Clotilde en traje de noche* (Room III)
- *Clotilde en traje gris* (Room III)
- Turkish bed, used by Sorolla for siestas (Room III)
- *La Siesta* (Room IV)
- *Las Velas* (Room IV)
- *Nadadores* (Room V)
- *Madre* (Room VI)
- New York gouaches (Drawings Room)

TIPS

- On Wednesday, the museum is open all day, right through lunchtime.
- The lovely gardens are a peaceful spot in bustling Madrid.

This serene spot belonged to Spain's finest Impressionist, Valencian Joaquín Sorolla, who wanted to create an oasis of peace for himself in a busy city. It is the best of Madrid's house museums.

Entrance and gardens The Sorolla Museum is one of the few places in the city to give us a sense of the shape of an artist's life and work. Built in 1910–11 by Enrique María de Repollés, it was the Madrid home of Joaquín Sorolla (1863–1923) and became a museum after Sorolla's widow, Clotilde, donated it to the state. It was opened to the public in 1932. The two small gardens, designed by Sorolla himself as a setting for his collection of fountains and fonts, are a bit of Andalucía in Madrid. The first is an imitation of a part of the Seville *alcázar*, while the second is

Statues in the beautiful gardens of Museo Sorolla (left and right)

modelled on the Generalife Gardens in Granada's Alhambra. Near the entrance is a replica of a white marble bust of Sorolla by Mariano Benlliure, and to the left is an Andalucian patio.

Inside Lovingly preserved, the house is redolent with turn-of-the-20th-century elegance. The ground floor, with its salon and dining room, gives a real feeling of the artist's life and displays his collection of antique pottery. The upper floor has been converted into a gallery, each room given over to a different aspect of Sorolla's work. Be sure to visit his studio, complete with a Turkish bed for the afternoon siesta. Among the paintings here are several of his wife, Clotilde. Although some see a fairy-tale, picture-postcard quality in his art, there is no denying the brilliance of his handling of light.

THE BASICS

http://museosorolla.
mcu.es

🚩 H4

✉ Paseo del General
Martínez Campos 37

☎ 91 310 15 84

🕐 Tue–Sat 9.30–8; closes
for lunch

🚇 Iglesia, Rubén Darío,
Gregorio Marañón

🚌 5, 14, 16, 27, 45, 61,
147, 150

💰 Inexpensive. Free to
under 18s, over 65s; Sun

♿ Few

More to See

BOTERO STATUES

In 1994, a section of Castellana was devoted to an exhibition of sculptures by 20th-century sculptor, Fernando Botero. When the exhibition ended, *madrileños* retained a *Hand* in the middle of Castellana; the *Reclining Woman* in Calle Génova; and *Man on a Mule* in the Plaza de Colón.

➕ G/H3 ✉ Plaza de San Juan de la Cruz 🚇 Colón, Nuevos Ministerios 🚌 7, 14, 27, 40, 147, 150

CASA DE LAS SIETE CHIMENEAS

Legend has it that Philip II built the House of the Seven Chimneys in the 1580s for one of his mistresses, who is said to haunt it. During restoration, a woman's skeleton was discovered with coins nearby from Philip II's time.

➕ G7 ✉ Plaza del Rey 🚇 Banco de España 🚌 1, 2, 74, 146

FUNDACIÓN JUAN MARCH

www.march.es

One of Europe's most important private art foundations, this is home to around 30 major annual exhibitions. Often among the most interesting to be found in Madrid, these have focused on Picasso, Kandinsky and Matisse.

➕ J5 ✉ Calle Castelló 77/Calle Padilla 36 ☎ 91 435 42 40 🕐 Mon–Sat 11–8, Sun and public hols 10–2. Closed Aug and between exhibitions. Free guided tours Wed 11, 2 and Fri 4.30, 7.30 🚇 Nuñez de Balboa 🚌 29, 52 ✋ Free ♿ Very good

IGLESIA DE SAN ANTÓN

Designed by Pedro Ribera and built by Juan de Villanueva, this example of baroque architecture houses a magnificent art collection, including Goya's *The Last Communion of Saint José de Calasanz*, painted between 1775 and 1780, and architect Ventura Rodríguez's *Dolphins* statue.

➕ G6 ✉ Hortaleza 63 ☎ 91 521 74 73 🚇 Tribunal, Chueca

MUSEO DE LA CIUDAD

The spacious Museum of the City opened in 1992 and is a high-tech equivalent of the Museo Municipal.

Museo de la Ciudad

The museum explains in almost numbing detail the workings of Madrid's roads and rail, telephone and water systems, and there are some attractive scale models and lots of interactive displays. There are often good temporary exhibitions.

➕ K2 ✉ Calle Principe de Vergara 140 ☎ 91 588 65 99 🕐 Tue–Fri 9.30–8, Sat, Sun 10–2 🚇 Cruz del Rayo 🚌 29, 52 💶 Free ❓ Guided tours can be arranged in advance ♿ Excellent

MUSEO DE ESCULTURA AL AIRE LIBRE

Connecting the *calles* Juan Bravo and Eduardo Dato is a road bridge over the Paseo de la Castellana. Underneath is an open-air display of sculpture by many of Spain's best-known contemporary artists.

➕ H4 ✉ Paseo de la Castellana 41 🚇 Rubén Darío 🚌 5, 14, 27, 37, 45

MUSEO ROMÁNTICO

www.museoromantico.mcu.es
This monument to faded romantic glory, founded in 1924, is inside a typical mid-18th-century *madrileño* building that was the home of the traveller-painter the Marqués de Véga-Inclán. Though the content—primarily 18th-century art—might be too sentimental for some, there are many items of interest, particularly Alenza's miniature *Satires of Romantic Suicide*, Goya's *Saint Gregory the Great*, and fine Isabelline and Imperial furniture.

➕ G6 ✉ Calle San Mateo 13 ☎ 91 448 10 45/91 448 01 63 🕐 Temporarily closed for restoration. Due to reopen in 2009, date to be announced, check at tourist information 🚇 Tribunal 🚌 21, 37 💶 Inexpensive. Free on Sun ♿ Very good

PASEO DE LA CASTELLANA

Running in an almost straight line from Colón for 6.5km (4 miles) to Plaza de Castilla, the Castellana is one of Madrid's main points of reference and a centre of business and nightlife. It splits the city in two, and many major sights are on or around it.

➕ H5 🚇 Colón, Rubén Darío, Nuevos Ministerios, Lima, Cuzco, Plaza de Castilla 🚌 5, 14, 27, 40, 45, 147, 149, 150

Museo Romántico

PLAZA DE DOS DE MAYO

2 May 1808 is one of the most famous dates in Madrid's history. It was during the French occupation and a 15-year-old girl, Manuela Malasaña, was shot by French soldiers for smuggling a weapon—a pair of scissors. Earlier in the day, two locals, Velarde and Daoiz, led an attack on the Monteléon artillery barracks (on the site of the present Dos de Mayo square) to capture arms. The insurgency was quashed, but sparked a four-year-long struggle for independence. The area is called Malasaña in memory of the heroine; the square bears the date of the revolt; and the arch in the middle of the square was the gate to the barracks. The dramatic statue here honours the two soldiers who died leading the uprising. Today, the square is lined with small bars and restaurants. Each year, on 2 May, one of Madrid's most popular annual festivals commemorates that fateful day, starting with parades and ending with a classical concert.

🚩 F5 🚇 Bilbao

SALA DEL CANAL DE ISABEL II

Considered one of Madrid's finest examples of industrial architecture, this display space, built in neo-Mudéjar style between 1907 and 1911, hosts frequent concerts and excellent art and photographic exhibitions.

🚩 F3 ✉ Calle Santa Engracia 125 ☎ 91 445 10 00 🕐 Tue–Sat 11–2, 5–8.30, Sun and public hols 11–2 🚇 Ríos Rosas 🚌 3, 37, 149 🖐 Free

SANTA BÁRBARA (LAS SALESAS REALES)

Probably the grandest, if not the most attractive, of Madrid's churches, Las Salesas was commissioned by Bárbara de Braganza, the wife of Fernando VI. It has an elaborate façade built between 1750 and 1758 by Carlier and Moradillo, and contains Sabatini's tomb of Fernando VI (1713–59). The adjoining monastery is currently the home of the Palacio de Justicia, or Supreme Court.

🚩 G6 ✉ Calle del General Castaños 2 ☎ 91 319 48 11 🕐 Daily 5–7pm; and for Mass 🚇 Alonso Martínez, Colón

Paseo de la Castellana (▷ 89)

A Walk North from Sol

Backstreets and boulevards, an arts centre and the up-and-coming area of Malasaña: all are part of this walk.

DISTANCE: 4.6km (2.8 miles) **ALLOW:** 3 hours

START

PUERTA DEL SOL
 F7 🚇 Sol

END

GRAN VÍA
 F7 🚇 Gran Vía

1 Leave the Puerta del Sol on the northwest side, on the pedestrianized Calle de Preciados. At the Plaza de Callao, bear left on the Gran Vía and follow it, past office blocks and cinemas, to the Plaza de España.

7 Exit the square on Calle de Velarde and walk to Calle de Fuencarral. Follow this past the Museo Municipal, currently under renovation, all the way down to Gran Vía.

2 Sit on a bench, enjoy the shade and pay your respects to Cervantes, Don Quixote and Sancho Panza, whose statues are at the far side of the square.

6 Turn right on Calle de Ruiz and walk down to the Plaza del Dos de Mayo. All around is the Malasaña area, whose little streets are full of tiny shops, bars and clubs.

5 Turn left on Calle de San Bernardo, walk uphill and cross over at the pedestrian crossing. Follow Calle de Divino Pastor, with its little old-fashioned shops and popular bars.

3 Now walk up the hill on the Calle de Princessa, into a more residential area. Cross over to the Plaza de Cristino Martos, walk through this small square and follow Calle de Conde Duque, past the huge Cultural Centre that used to be an army barracks.

4 Turn right on Calle de Montserrat, immediately right on Calle de Amaniel and stroll through the Plaza de las Comendadoras. Exit the little square on Calle de Quiñones.

Shopping

ABC SERRANO SHOPPING CENTRE

www.abcserrano.com

The tiled exterior of what were the ABC newspaper offices now hides an Aladdin's cave of boutiques. With over 60 to choose from, this is a place to relax and check out the baby clothes and wine, the high fashion and fun jewellery. Good restaurants on site.

✚ H4/5 ✉ Calle de Serrano 61/Castellana 34 ☎ 91 577 50 31 🚇 Rubén Dario, Nuñez de Balboa, Serrano

CACAO SAMPAKA

www.cacaosampaka.com

This could be Madrid's most tempting shop. Sampaka sells bars of chocolate as other shops sell silk ties. But it is not just bars. There are books and biscuits, jars and moulds, drinking chocolate and decorations. And the bar-cum-tasting room serves chocolate drinks, mousses, pastries and desserts.

✚ H6 ✉ Calle de Orellana 4 ☎ 91 319 58 40 🚇 Alonso Martínez

GUITARRAS JAVIER

Despite Madrid's youth-oriented fashion craze, there are still traditional crafts. For over 50 years, Javier Rojo Solar has been making superb guitars and other stringed instruments at his shop-cum-workshop. Maestros such as Narciso Yepes have been his customers.

✚ F5 ✉ Calle del Divino Pastor 22 ☎ 91 445 72 19 🚇 Bilbao, San Bernardo

HOMELESS

www.homeless.es

This boutique was founded in 1994 in San Sebastian as a fund-raising venture for the homeless. It now has its own label, 'HOSS'. The designs are casual, but stylish, aimed mainly at young professionals. There's another branch in the Salamanca district (Calle Serrano 16).

✚ F6/7 ✉ Calle Fuencarral 16 ☎ 91 524 17 28 🚇 Gran Via

IOLI

Leather shoes and bags, silk hats and purses, all in vivid colours, all designed and made by Cynthia Ioli,

the Argentine owner of this tiny shop. Women's shoes can be made to measure.

✚ F6 ✉ Calle del Espiritu Santo 1 ☎ 91 521 00 22 🚇 Tribunal

MERCADO DE FUENCARRAL

www.mdf.es/madrid

Three floors and an outside area dedicated to the youth market. If you are looking for something out of the ordinary in fashion, leisure and culture, this is it: live DJs, hairdressers, tattoo parlours and loads of clothing, jewellery and gifts.

✚ F6 ✉ Calle de Fuencarral 45 ☎ 91 521 41 52 🚇 Tribunal, Chueca, Gran Via

PURIFICACIÓN GARCÍA

www.purificationgarcia.es

The sleek look, one of the trademarks of this distinguished Spanish designer of prêt-à-porter men's and women's clothing, is reflected in the minimalist layout of the store.

✚ E8 ✉ Calle de Serrano 28 and 92 ☎ 91 435 80 13/576 72 76 🚇 Serrano

RESERVA Y CATA

www.reservaycata.com

Don't miss this *bodega* (wine store) in a Chueca basement, offering 600 different wines of mainly Spanish origin.

✚ G6 ✉ Calle de Conde de Xiquena 13 ☎ 91 319 04 01 🚇 Colón

Entertainment and Nightlife

AREIA COLONIAL CHILL OUT
www.areiachillout.com
The place to relax where DJs perform nightly; cocktails and exotic snacks, too.
⊞ G6 ✉ Calle de Hortaleza 92 ☎ 91 310 03 07
◷ 1pm–3pm Ⓜ Tribunal

BAR CAFÉ DEL FORO
Though it does stage straight rock, the Café del Foro also has salsa, fusion and cabaret. Friendly and buzzing venue.
⊞ F5 ✉ Calle San Andrés 38 ☎ 91 445 37 52 Ⓜ Bilbao

BUHO REAL
www.buhoreal.com
You might see the next big up-and-coming international act here at the 'Royal Owl'.
⊞ G6 ✉ Calle Regueros 5 ☎ 91 308 48 51
◷ Concerts start at 9.30pm, closing times vary Ⓜ Alonso Martinez

CAFÉ MANUELA
After being wowed by the décor, visitors usually find the congenial atmosphere here well suited to writing postcards or chatting to friends. Occasional live entertainment—music concerts, poetry readings, exhibitions by local artists.
⊞ F6 ✉ San Vincente Ferrer 29 ☎ 91 531 70 37
Ⓜ Tribunal

CAFÉ LA PALMA
www.cafelapalma.com
A cross between a conventional café, a wine bar, a Moroccan tea shop and a nightclub. The music in La Palma is just as eclectic too—everything from rock 'n' roll to flamenco and Cuban fusion.
⊞ F6 ✉ Calle de la Palma 62 ☎ 91 522 50 31 ◷ Daily from 4pm Ⓜ Noviciado

CAFÉ RUIZ
A relatively peaceful retreat from the night-time mayhem of surrounding Malasaña, the Ruiz retains a late 19th-century feel and serves cocktails as well as coffee and milkshakes.
⊞ F5 ✉ Calle Ruiz 11 ☎ 91 446 12 32 Ⓜ Bilbao

EL CLANDESTINO
Close to the Plaza de Chueca, this may look like just another small night club, but it has a reputation for showcasing great bands for its live music, usually jazz.
⊞ G6 ✉ Calle del Barquillo 43 ☎ 91 521 55 63

CHUPITO
Don't be surprised if, at the end of a meal in a restaurant, your waiter offers you a *chupito*. Usually served in a shot glass, a *chupito* is small but strong: *orujo de hierbas* (a yellow or green herb liquor), *ponche caballero* (spiced orange brandy), *pacharán* (sloe gin). This is on the house, helps to digest the meal and sends you on your way in a happy frame of mind.

◷ Thu–Sat 1pm–3am
Ⓜ Chueca

DEL DIEGO
Del Diego's superb design and highly attentive bar staff have quickly made it one of Madrid's big three *coctelerías*, along with El Chicote and Le Cock, two minutes away. This is the place to be or be seen.
⊞ G7 ✉ Calle de la Reina 12 ☎ 91 523 31 06
Ⓜ Gran Vía

FORTUNY
www.jardinfortuny.net
Glitzy nightclub where you might bump into media celebrities. The terrace garden is the best feature of this former palace, which also has a reputable restaurant. Strict dress code.
⊞ H4 ✉ Calle de Fortuny 34 ☎ 91 319 05 88
◷ Closed lunch Sat, Sun in winter Ⓜ Bilbao

OJALÁ AWARENESS CLUB
A typical example of the café clubs in Malasaña, this is fun upstairs (movies projected onto walls) and even more fun downstairs, where sand on the floor re-creates summer beach parties, complete with low seats and cushions. Drinks and snacks all day; dinner in the evening.
⊞ F6 ✉ Calle de San Andrés 1 ☎ 91 523 27 47 ◷ 11am–midnight, later at weekends
Ⓜ Noviciado, Tribunal

Restaurants

CHUECA AND THE NORTH

Prices are approximate,
based on a 3-course
meal for one person.
€€€   over €45
€€   €25–€45
€   under €25

EL 4 DE TAPAS (€)

www.4detapas.com
A mix of bar and restaurant in Chueca, this is the place for a crowd that cannot make up its mind: from tapas, salads and peppers stuffed with *bacalao* to pasta and grilled meat, the menu has something for everyone. The setting is modern, with music.

🔲 G7 ✉ Calle de Barbieri 4
☎ 91 523 94 64 🕐 Daily
🚇 Chueca, Gran Vía

BAJO CERO (€)

www.bajocero.es
Madrid has gone mad for an Argentine ice-cream parlour (Bajo Cero means Below Zero), with a design-conscious, lounge-like setting. Order the Giangrossi hand-made ice cream or a pastry, then settle in with your laptop.

🔲 F4 ✉ Glorieta Quevedo 6
☎ 902 11 33 77 🕐 Mon–Thu 8am–midnight, Fri 8am–2am, Sat 10am–2am, Sun 10am–midnight 🚇 Quevedo

BAZTÁN (€)

An ideal spot to learn more about Spain's best wines, this is a new bar in an old *taberna*, overlooking the historic Plaza del Dos de Mayo. Tapas and other well-prepared snacks.

🔲 F5 ✉ Calle de San Andrés 14 ☎ 91 523 25 73
🕐 Noon–midnight, later at weekends. Closed Mon
🚇 Tribunal, Bilbao

NINA MADRID (€€)

With bare brick walls, this is Madrid's answer to the New York look. Always busy, still fashionable, Nina's chefs create Mediterranean-style dishes using seasonal herbs and vegetables, with top-quality fish and meat. Solid Spanish wine list. Good weekend brunch (12.30 to 5.30pm).

🔲 F5 ✉ Calle de Manuela Malasaña 10 ☎ 91 591 00 46
🕐 Daily 🚇 Bilbao

When in Rome…aperitifs still whet the appetite in Spain. Try *vermut* (vermouth), often served on draft from a barrel in many tapas bars. Particularly popular before lunch, vermouth is made from wine infused with herbs and makes an excellent accompaniment for tapas. Order a *vermut con sifón*, with soda, for a refreshing long drink. Sherry is the other great aperitif: *fino* (pale and dry), *manzanilla* (also dry), *amontillado* (a rich, nutty, mature *fino*), *palo cortado* (a rare sherry, between dry and medium), and *oloroso* (rich, but can be dry or sweet).

PEDRO LARUMBE (€€€)

www.larumbe.com
On the top floor of the ABC Serrano, this restaurant is theatrical and luxurious, ideal for that special occasion. Well-known chef Pedro Larumbe uses lobster and asparagus, foie gras and duck for the well-heeled clientele who live nearby. Well-priced wines.

🔲 H4/5 ✉ Calle de Serrano 61, 4th floor ☎ 91 575 11 12
🕐 Closed Sat lunch, Sun
🚇 Rubén Dario, Nuñez de Balboa, Serrano

EL PLACER DEL ESPÍRITU SANTO (€)

www.elplacerdelespiritusanto.com
Typical of the new breed of Spanish cooking, this is a small buzzy restaurant where traditional dishes are given a modern twist: pumpkin ravioli with a tomato and mint sauce, beef cheeks with vanilla, feather-light tiramisu.

🔲 F6 ✉ Calle del Espíritu Santo 3 ☎ 91 360 45 16
🕐 Closed Sun dinner, Mon
🚇 Tribunal

LA SACRISTÍA (€€)

This restaurant is popular with local actors and directors, and is particularly well-known for its *bacalao* (cod) dishes. It also serves excellent steaks and *gambas* flamed in whisky.

🔲 G7 ✉ Calle de las Infantas 28 ☎ 91 522 09 45
🕐 Closed Sun 🚇 Gran Vía

To the north of central Madrid are two of the city's great stadiums, the bullring and Real Madrid football club's Bernabéu Stadium. And within an hour or so of the city are some of the most historic and beautiful cities in Spain.

Sights	98–102	Top 25	**25**
Excursions	103–106	Plaza de Toros ▷ **98**
		Real Madrid ▷ **100**

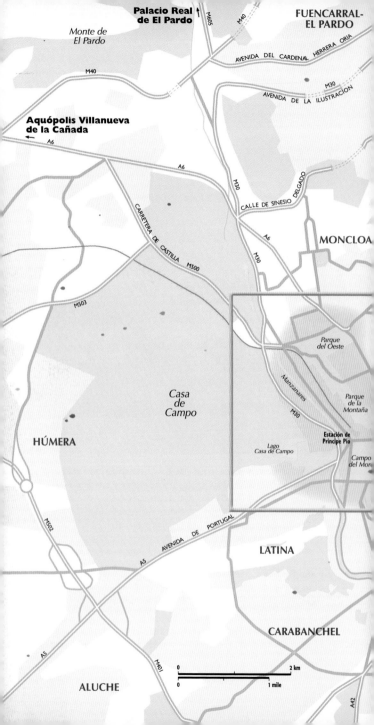

Cuatro Torres Business Area

M607

M40

AVENIDA MANUEL AZAÑA

M30

Estación de Chamartín

Puerta de Europa (Torres Kio)

TETUÁN

Real Madrid Estadio Santiago Bernabéu

CHAMARTIN

AVENIDA DE LA PAZ

Aquópolis San Fernando de Henares, Los Caprichos Alameda de Osuna

PASEO DE LA CASTELLANA

AVENIDA DE AMÉRICA

A2

Aeroporto de Madrid-Barajas

M30

CHAMBERÍ

Plaza de Toros

M110

SALAMANCA

PASEO DE LA CASTELLANA

Parque Quinta Fuente del Berro

MADRID

Parque del Retiro

RETIRO

M23

AVENIDA DE LA PAZ

M30

CENTRO

Faunia

A3/E901

AVENIDA DEL MEDITERRÁNEO

Estación de Atocha

ARGANZUELA

M30

Parque Cerro del Tío Pío

Parque Enrique Tierno Galvan

M203

M30

PUENTE VALLECAS

Estación Entrevías

USERA

A4/E05

Warner Bros Park

Plaza de Toros

TOP 25

Plaza de Toros (left); spectators watching a bullfight (right); a matador (opposite)

FARTHER AFIELD   TOP 25

THE BASICS

www.las-ventas.com

➕ M5

✉ Avenida de los Toreros, Calle de Alcalá 237

☎ Museum 91 725 18 57; Stadium 91 356 22 00

🕐 Museo Taurino: Mar–Oct Tue–Fri 9.30–2.30, Sun, public hols 10–1; Nov–Feb Mon–Fri 9.30–2.30

🚇 Ventas

🚌 12, 21, 38, 106, 110, 146

💷 Museo Taurino free

❓ Take a 40-min tour of the bullring, Tue–Sun 10–2. English spoken, €5

♿ None

HIGHLIGHTS

● Bullfighting costumes in the museum – 'suits of lights' may contain 5kg (11 pounds) of gold embroidery
● A papal bull in the museum (1567), which bans bullfighting
● *Portrait of Joaquín de Rodrigo*, attributed to Goya
● Highlight of the season is in May, during the *Feria San Isidro*, when some 30 bull-fights take place

Is bullfighting art or blood sport? Whatever your feelings, you cannot help but be impressed by the world's most important bullring, the place in which a bullfighter must triumph if he is to achieve international recognition.

History and architecture The 1930s bullring is Madrid's finest example of neo-Mudéjar architecture, a style that resurfaced during the 19th century in imitation of the Mudéjar architecture of the 13th and 14th centuries and is defined by an interesting use of brickwork and attractive, bright ceramic tile inlay. In the square in front of the bullring is a melodramatic statue in memory of bullfighter José Cubero, inscribed with the words 'a bullfighter died, and an angel was born.'

Museo Taurino Half an hour in the stuffy Museo Taurino, next to the stables, gives you a basic overview of the famous names in bullfighting, if not of the complex art of bullfighting itself. Massive heads of legendary bulls and portraits of great bullfighters line the walls, and there are several dramatic portrayals of bull-runs, including a notable one by Mariano Benlliure (1868–1947). The highlights are the *trajes de luces* (suits of lights), as they are known, among them one belonging to Juanita Cruz, an early-20th-century woman bullfighter who was never allowed to fight on Spanish soil, and another worn by Manolete, perhaps the greatest of them all, who died in the ring in 1947. The museum displays are labelled in both Spanish and English.

Real Madrid

El Estadio Santiago Bernabéu is Real Madrid's home ground

THE BASICS

www.realmadrid.com

⊞ H1

✉ Calle Conche Espina 1

☎ Stadium: 91 398 43 70; tickets: 902 31 17 09

🕐 Guided tours in English from Gate 7, Mon–Sat 10–7, Sun, public hols 10.30–6.30. No tours 5 hours before match. Sala de Trofeos Tue–Sun 10.30–7.30; closed 3 hours before match

🍴 Café on site

🚇 Santiago Bernabéu

🚌 14

💶 Tour expensive, trophy room moderate

♿ Good

Founded in 1902, 'Real'—or Royal—rose to become one of the world's most famous football clubs. Its impressive achievements were officially recognized by FIFA, the world governing body, in 1988, when it was awarded the accolade, 'the best club in the history of football'.

El Estadio Santiago Bernabéu Real Madrid have their home in the Santiago Bernabéu stadium. The stadium was inaugurated as the Estadio Chamartín (after the old stadium) in 1947, but the name was changed in 1955 in honour of the club's president. Today it holds more than 80,000 spectators, although before UEFA ruled that all standing places had to be converted to seats it held well over 100,000. In 1982, the stadium had perhaps its greatest hour, when it hosted the World Cup Final (when Italy beat Germany 3–1).

HIGHLIGHTS

● The massive world-famous stadium

● The Trophy Room, with its World and European silverware

● The new Realcafé Bernabéu, with its views

● Any home match, with passionate fans

● The club shop, with its array of replica shirts

● The stadium tour

Museum Even if you can't get to a game, you can take a guided tour of the stadium. You will get to enjoy a panoramic view of the inside of the stadium, the pitch and players' tunnel, the away dressing room and the Trophy Room. Unsurprisingly, given the club's illustrious history, this is packed with silver trophies. Numerous video screens show clips from great matches of the past, including *los blancos'* record nine European Cup triumphs between 1956 and 2006, as well as 17 Spanish cups and 31 Spanish League championships. Success is not limited to football: Real participates in many sports, notably basketball.

More to See

AQUÓPOLIS

www.aquopolis.es

Spanish children beg their parents to take them to Aquópolis, the biggest and best of the Madrid water parks and one of the largest in Europe. There are huge water slides, an adventure lake and wave machines. There is another Aquópolis, at San Fernando de Henares, 15km (9 miles) east of Madrid. There are rides, a lake and plenty of trees for shade.

🛨 Off map 🖂 Villanueva de la Cañada. Carretera de El Escorial km25 ☎ 902 34 50 06 🕒 Jun, Sep 12–7; Jul–Aug 12–8 🍴 Cafés 💷 Expensive
At San Fernando de Henares: 🛨 Off map 🖂 Carretera Nacional II ☎ 902 34 50 22 🕒 Jun, Sep 12–7; Jul–Aug 12–8 💷 Expensive

LOS CAPRICHOS DE ALAMEDA DE OSUNA

This is the closest Madrid comes to a formal English garden. Though a fair distance out, it's pleasant for Sunday strolls.
🛨 Off map 🖂 Paseo de la Alameda de Osuna 🚇 Canillejas

CUATRO TORRES BUSINESS AREA

A line of four stunning skyscrapers dominates the northern part of the city. Two of them, Torre Caja de Madrid and Torre de Cristal, are the two tallest buildings in Spain, each 250m (820ft). The towers can be seen from the entrance/exit to the Metro at Chamartin station.
🛨 Off map 🖂 Paseo de la Castellana 🚇 Chamartín, Begoña

FAUNIA

www.faunia.es

Europe's only theme park dedicated to nature and biodiversity. The eight pavilions, each of which re-creates a different ecosystem with the authentic sights, sounds, smells, flora and fauna, will amaze and delight. Experience a tropical rainstorm and find out what it's like to live in the Arctic.
🛨 Off map 🖂 Avenida de las Comunidades 28 ☎ 91 301 62 35 🕒 Open daily from 10am; hours vary according to season and day of week. Check 🍴 Cafés 🚇 Valdebernardo 💷 Expensive

Water-park fun

PALACIO REAL DE EL PARDO

www.patrimonionacional.es

Set in a vast park northwest of the city, this former royal palace is usually referred to as El Pardo, after the hill where it stands. Originally a hunting lodge back in 1405, the palace was built for Carlos I and expanded by Carlos III and his architect, Sabatini, in the 18th century. It was home to General Franco for 35 years. Today, you can visit rooms decorated with fine tapestries designed by Goya and woven at the Real Fábrica de Tapices (▷ 77), as well as murals by Maella and Bayeu. Not to be confused with the nearby Palacio de la Zarzuela, the home of the Spanish royal family since 1962, which is not open to the public.

🔛 Off map 🖂 Calle Manuel Alonso, El Pardo ☎ 91 376 15 00 🕐 Winter: Mon–Sat 10.30–4.45, Sun, public hols 10–1.30. Summer: Mon–Sat 10.30–5.45, Sun, hols 9.30–1.30 🍴 Restaurants nearby 🏷 Moderate. Free Wed EU citizens 🚌 Línea Interurbana 60. By car 14km (8.5 miles) from central Madrid via the M-30, M-605

PUERTA DE EUROPA (TORRES KIO)

These striking towers are named after the Kuwaiti Investment Office, which withdrew funding halfway through construction. The walls are angled inwards at 15 degrees—more than that and they would collapse.

🔛 Off map 🖂 Plaza de Castilla 🚇 Plaza de Castilla 🚌 5, 27, 42, 124, 125, 147, 149

WARNER BROS PARK

www.parquewarner.com

This huge theme park on the outskirts of Madrid opened in 2003. The five zones are all themed: Cartoon Village, Hollywood Boulevard, the Old West, Super Heroes and Warner Studios. Recent attractions include the family roller coaster ride, Correcaminos Bip Bip, and Yogi Bear in Polynesia.

🔛 Off map 🖂 San Martín de La Vega. NIV to km22, then M-506 and follow signs ☎ 902 02 41 00 🕐 Hours vary from winter to summer (only open weekends in winter) and from day to day and month to month so always check first 🍴 Cafés, restaurants 🚆 C3 from Atocha 🏷 Expensive

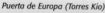

Puerta de Europa (Torres Kio)

EL ESCORIAL

Philip II's vast palace and monastery was built between 1563 and 1584 as his mausoleum. Apart from its political pedigree, it's also an architectural triumph, with impressive collections of objects and antiques.

The palace contains 16 courtyards, 2,673 windows, 1,200 doors and 86 staircases; 900m (2,952ft) of frescoes line the walls. Its power is breathtaking, and the clear mountain air has left its granite and blue roof slates looking extraordinarily new. Among the highlights are the monastery, the library and the mausoleum, the resting place of most Spanish monarchs since Charles V (1500–58).

THE BASICS

www.patrimonionacional.es
Distance: 60km (37 miles)
Journey time: 1 hour
☎ 91 890 59 02/03
🕐 Apr–Sep Tue–Sun 10–6; Oct–Mar 10–5 (last admission 1 hour before closing)
🚉 Regular trains from Atocha
💷 Expensive: €10 with guide, €8 without guide. Free Wed for EU citizens

SEGOVIA

Segovia, perched on a lofty, rocky outcrop, was founded during the Iberian period and taken by the Romans in 80BC. Occupied by the Moors, it then reverted to the Christians in 1085, and now, a millennium later, is a popular weekend destination for *madrileños* in search of fresh air and a traditional suckling pig lunch.

The first thing you will see is the Roman aqueduct (1st and 2nd centuries AD), with 165 arches and a total length of 814m (2,670ft). In the old town are the magnificent 16th-century cathedral, with its imposing flying buttresses, and the 14th-century Alcázar, or fortress, which was largely rebuilt as a Gothic fantasy in the 19th century and offers lovely views from the top. Segovia is well known as the capital of Castillian cuisine.

THE BASICS

www.segoviaturismo.com
Distance: 88km (55 miles)
Journey time: 2 hours
🚌 La Sepulvedana bus line from Paseo de la Florida 11, near Príncipe Pío Metro station
🚉 From Chamartín station (very slow)
🍴 Candido, Plaza Azoguejo 5
ℹ️ Plaza Mayor 10 (tel 921 46 03 04); Plaza Azoguejo (tel 921 46 67 70). From Plaza Azoguejo, free guided tours of the city in Spanish (English leaflet) Jul–Sep (but you must pay the entry fee to the monuments)

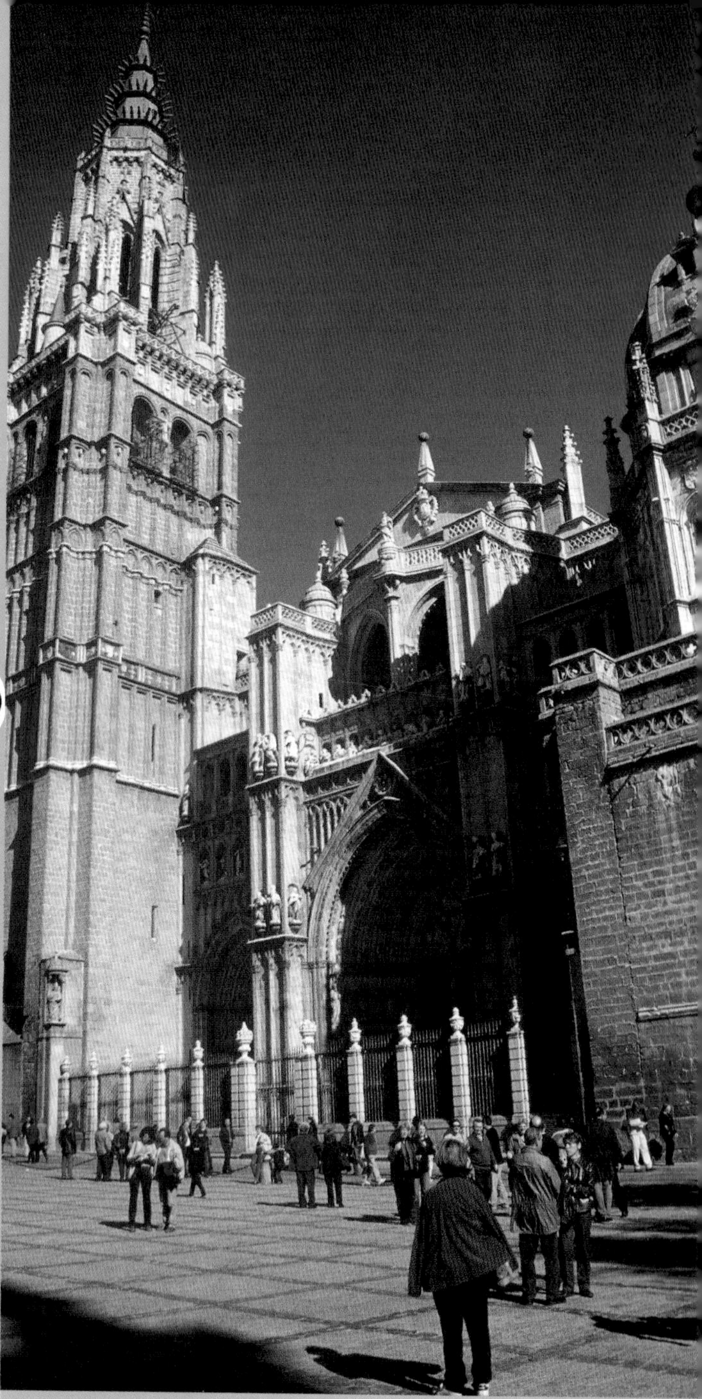

TOLEDO

Legendary Toledo, with its hilltop site and fascinating maze of winding streets and hidden patios, is one of the nation's most beautiful and legendary cities. It was the Spanish capital from 567 to 711, and from 1085 to 1561. In other words, it has played a decisive role in Spanish history for far longer than Madrid.

National Monument Between the 12th and 15th centuries, Moors, Jews and Christians lived here side by side, and its rich combination of Moorish, Christian and Jewish heritage inspired its designation as a National Monument. Highlights are the 13th-century cathedral, the synagogues, Santo Tomé, the Museo de la Santa Cruz (for El Greco paintings) and the Alcázar, founded in 1085.

Alcázar Every culture that has ruled Toledo built a fortress on this site, and all dominated the city's skyline, as does the present-day version. This rather austere fortress was built by Charles V in the 16th century. During the Civil War, owing to its strategic position, it endured a very destructive 70-day siege, and today it houses an army museum that concentrates on those dark days.

Catedral Toledo's cathedral, one of the world's finest Gothic buildings, took 267 years to erect (1226–1493). Among its treasures are a baroque marble, jasper and bronze altarpiece, and paintings by El Greco and Goya.

Judería Although only two of Toledo's original 10 synagogues stand today, there is still a surprising amount to see in the Jewish Quarter. The 14th-century Sinagoga del Tránsito, housing the Museo Sefardí, has a superb Mudéjar interior.

THE BASICS

www.toledo-turismo.com
Distance: 70km (45 miles)
Journey time: 1 hour 15 mins
🚌 Galeano International from Estación Sur, Méndez Álvaro
🚆 From Atocha, several every hour in summer, less frequent in winter. To avoid a steep climb take a bus up the hill
🛈 Plaza del Consistorio 1 (tel 925 25 40 30). Open daily 10–6. You can take a guided electric car or Segway tour. E-tur: tel 925 01 56 65; www.e-tur.es

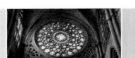

THE BASICS

www.aranjuez.com
Distance: 50km (31 miles)
Journey time: 1 hour
🚌 Estación Sur, Méndez Álvaro (tel 91 468 22 00)
🚆 Atocha (tel 902 24 02 02)
ℹ️ Plaza de San Antonio (tel 91 891 04 27). Open Tue–Sun 10–2, 4–6 (summer); 10–1, 3–5 (winter)

Palacio Real
☎ 91 891 07 40
🕐 Daily 10–6.15 (summer); 10–5.15 (winter). Closed Mon
💶 Moderate. Free Wed for EU citizens

❓ A special Strawberry Train (Tren de la Fresa) runs on weekends from Madrid, from late April through June. The train departs from Atocha train station at 10.05, arriving in Aranjuez at 11; the return journey departs around 6pm. The ticket price includes a guided visit of the palace and gardens, as well as a bowl of strawberries en route (tel 902 22 88 22)

ARANJUEZ

An hour south of Madrid is a city known as much for a piece of classical guitar music as for its glorious royal palace. On the banks of the Tajo River, Aranjuez is green, leafy and cool.

Palacio Real This lush landscape inspired Joaquín Rodrigo (1901–99) to compose the romantic and hugely popular *Concierto de Aranjuez*. (He is buried in the town cemetery.) The setting also drew Spanish rulers from the heat of Madrid. Although Felipe II commissioned the first palace back in 1561, the Palacio Real de Aranjuez took ages to finish: what you see is from the 18th century. But this fairy-tale palace was well worth the wait, from the throne room with its red velvet to the gala dining hall with its impressive chandeliers, furniture, tapestries and sculptures. One vast room, the Sala de Porcelana, is filled with porcelain, a particular hobby of Carlos III. Outstanding works of art include Murillo's *Bautismo de Cristo* (*Baptism of Christ*), which covers the ceiling of the chapel.

Gardens Many gardening enthusiasts go to Aranjuez just to see the landscaped grounds around the palace, with their fountains, statues and walks: the Jardín del Príncipe (Prince's Garden), the Jardín de Isabel II, the Jardín de la Isla (the Island) and the Jardín del Parterre, designed by Boutelou in 1746, with fine cedar trees, magnolias and flowers.

Strawberries But the whole town is a pleasure to visit, with its old houses and small palaces, many of which are still in private hands. The town is also famous for its strawberries: a day trip to Aranjuez to eat strawberries is a Madrid tradition.

On a budget or celebrating a special event? With family or just looking for a fun weekend away? Even if you want to stay right in the throbbing heart of Madrid, there is accommodation for all wallets.

Introduction   **108**

Budget Hotels   **109**

Mid-Range Hotels   **110–111**

Luxury Hotels   **112**

Introduction

Spain's capital has a wealth of hotels, *pensiones* and *hostales*. If you arrive without a booking, there are accommodation services at the airport and main bus and train stations. Many upper-range hotels, geared to business travel, offer reduced rates at weekends and holiday periods, so it's worth asking about reductions.

Location

The main factor to think about is location. The most popular area for visitors is in the heart of the old town (south of Sol between Plaza Mayor and Plaza de Santa Ana); you can walk to many of the main sights from here. Other options include Recoletos, the Paseo del Prado or Salamanca. If you want to be right in the heart of the nightlife action, Malasaña and Chueca are good bets.

Types of Accommodation

Spanish hotels are classified, regularly inspected and awarded 1 to 5 stars (*estrellas*). *Hostales* are often hard to distinguish from small hotels and can be better value for money. They are graded from 1 to 3 stars; a 3-star *hostal* is generally on a par with a 2-star hotel. *Pensiones* are usually family-run with simple rooms and sometimes shared bathrooms. Larger establishments have their own restaurants but in smaller places you'll need to eat out. If you prefer self-catering, you can also hire apartments from €50 a night for one person; see websites such as gomadrid.com or madridman.com. It's worth paying for a room with air-conditioning; summer temperatures can exceed 40ºC (104ºF).

DISABLED ACCESS

Look for modern hotels if you require better access and specially adapted rooms (www.access-able.com). These range from the well-priced Ibis Centro, with two disabled rooms (www.ibis.com), to the luxury InterContinental Madrid (four rooms, www.ichotelsgroup.com). The website www.laterooms.com lists rooms for people with disabilities. In Spanish, look for the word *minusválido* (disabled).

Budget Hotels

BARBIERI INTERNATIONAL HOSTEL

www.barbierihostel.com

A backpackers' hostel (all ages welcome) near Plaza de Chueca, which provides accommodation in shared rooms of 2, 4 and 8 beds. Bathrooms are single sex. Other services include 24-hour reception and kitchen facilities.

➕ G6 ✉ Calle Barbieri 15 (2nd floor) ☎ 91 531 02 58 🚇 Chueca, Gran Vía

GALIANO RESIDENCIA

www.hotelgaliano.com

In a quiet location, the Galiano's 29 spacious rooms and old-world feel make it one of Madrid's better-kept secrets.

➕ H5/6 ✉ Calle de Alcalá Galiano 6 ☎ 91 319 20 00 🚇 Colón

HOSTAL ALASKA

www.hostalalaska.com

A *hostal* on the fourth floor of a building in a relatively quiet street off the Puerta del Sol. It offers seven en-suite rooms with heating and air-conditioning. Free Wi-Fi access.

➕ F7 ✉ Calle Espoz y Mina 7 (4th floor) ☎ 91 521 18 45 🚇 Sol

HOSTAL CERVANTES

www.hostal-cervantes.com

Conveniently located on the street after which it is named, an easy walk from the Prado and Thyssen-Bornemisza. The 20 en-suite rooms have televisions, safes and hairdryers. Rooms can be reserved online.

➕ G8 ✉ Calle Cervantes 34 ☎ 91 429 83 65 🚇 Anton Martín, Banco de España

HOTEL RESIDENCIA PAZ

Some rooms of this *hostal*, on a quiet street, overlook a shady courtyard. It's very clean, very efficient and very friendly.

➕ E7 ✉ Calle Flora 4 (2nd floor) ☎ 91 547 30 47 🚇 Sol, Ópera

IBIS MADRID CENTRO

www.ibishotel.com

On the site of a famous theatre, this is a practical and friendly 64-room hotel in Malasaña, one of the up-and-coming areas of the city. A good base, with plenty of restaurants and bars nearby. Excellent breakfasts.

➕ F5 ✉ Calle de Manuela Malasaña 6 ☎ 91 448 58 16 🚇 Bilbao

OLÉ INTERNATIONAL HOSTEL

www.olehostel.com

This Malasaña hostel

THINGS TO NOTE

It is worth remembering that, at the lower end of the scale, a good *hostal* may be more comfortable than a poor hotel. Remember: prices can vary according to season.

(open 24 hours) has a good kitchen, common room with satellite TV and internet, and lockers for valuables. Linen and breakfast are included and towels are available.

➕ F5 ✉ Calle Manuela Malasaña 23, (1st floor) ☎ 91 446 51 65 🚇 Bilbao, San Bernardo

SAN LORENZO

www.hotel-sanlorenzo.com

The San Lorenzo is most notable for its soundproof windows. Décor is stylish and rooms comfortable.

➕ G7 ✉ Calle Clavel 8 ☎ 91 521 30 57 🚇 Gran Vía

SANTANDER

www.hotelsantandermadrid.com

An old building decorated in the classical style. Rooms are en-suite and have heating and air-conditioning. No meals served but there are restaurants all around.

➕ G7 ✉ Calle Echegaray 1 (corner with Carrera de San Jerónimo 26) ☎ 91 429 95 51 🚇 Sol, Sevilla

TRAFALGAR

www.bestwesternhoteltrafalgar.com

The Trafalgar, in a residential area north of the centre, is excellent value. All 48 rooms are nicely decorated in modern style and equipped with satellite TV. There's a restaurant, bar and an indoor swimming pool.

➕ F4 ✉ Calle Trafalgar 35 ☎ 91 445 62 00 🚇 Iglesia

Mid-Range Hotels

PRICES

Expect to pay between €100 and €175 per night for two in a mid-range room.

ACIS Y GALATEA
www.acisygalatea.com
A small (20-room), tasteful, strikingly modern hotel some distance from the city hub in the direction of the airport and near the IFEMA international trade fair showground. The name and the interior decorating theme are inspired by opera. Wi-Fi internet throughout.
➕ Off map ✉ Calle Galatea 6 ☎ 91 743 49 01
🚇 Canillejas

AROSA
www.hotelarosa.com
Very central, the 139-room Arosa has long been popular, particularly with families, and makes an excellent base.
➕ F7 ✉ Calle de la Salud 21 ☎ 91 532 16 00 🚇 Sol, Gran Vía

ASTURIAS
www.cch.es/asturias
Convenient to the Puerta del Sol, the 175-room Asturias is close to the main sights and nightlife. Ask for an inside room if you're sensitive to noise.
➕ G7 ✉ Calle Sevilla 2 ☎ 91 429 66 76 🚇 Sevilla

CARLOS V
www.bestwesternhotelcarlosv.com
The 67-room Carlos V is clean and bright and is next to the Puerto del Sol. If you can get a room on the sixth floor, you will get a balcony.
➕ F7 ✉ Calle Maestro Victoria 5 ☎ 91 531 41 00 🚇 Sol

CONDE DUQUE
www.hotelcondeduque.es
Located in an enclosed square, the 143-room Conde Duque is among the more peaceful hotels near the city centre.
➕ F5 ✉ Plaza del Conde Valle Suchil 5 ☎ 91 447 70 00 🚇 San Bernardo

EUROPA
A comfortable hotel in a good location right on the Puerto del Sol, and within easy walking distance of the main sights.
➕ F7 ✉ Calle del Carmen 4 ☎ 91 521 29 00 🚇 Callao

GREEN EL PRADO
www.pradohotel.com
In this lovely building, within easy reach of the Prado and the Santa Ana district, windows are double-glazed, ensuring a good night's sleep.
➕ G8 ✉ Calle Prado 11

RESERVATIONS

Madrid has many hotels, and finding a room should not be hard except in tourist areas. Book as far in advance as possible, and call to re-confirm. If you arrive without a reservation, contact a tourist information office.

☎ 91 369 02 34 🚇 Antón Martín, Sevilla

HOTEL T3 TIROL
www.t3tirol.com
A comfortable hotel in the middle of the Argüelles business district. It has recently been renovated and it now also caters to families with small kids. Keen shoppers will find this location convenient, as the El Corte Inglés department store is just opposite; Parque del Oeste is also nearby. Hotel amenities include parking, internet access and car rental facilities.
➕ D5 ✉ Calle Marqués de Urquijo 4 ☎ 91 548 19 00 🚇 Argüelles

INGLÉS
www.hotel-ingles.net
The clean, 58-room, family-owned Inglés is pleasantly located in a maze of narrow streets within easy reach of many sights. Good value.
➕ G7 ✉ Calle Echegaray 8 ☎ 91 429 65 51 🚇 Sevilla

LAGASCA
www.nh-hotels.com
This 3-star hotel in the heart of the Salamanca district is near the Calle Serrano shops and a host of good restaurants. It was opened in the early 1990s and its 100 rooms are plainly furnished with wooden floors and striking bathrooms. It also has parking.
➕ J5 ✉ Calle de Lagasca 64 ☎ 91 575 40 06
🚇 Velázquez, Serrano

MEDIODÍA

www.mediodiahotel.com
Opposite Atocha train station, the Mediodía is close to the Reina Sofía and the Prado, and is well connected by public transport. Rooms are spacious and simple and have private bathrooms.
⊞ H9 ⊠ Plaza Emperador Carlos V 8 ☎ 91 527 30 60 🚇 Atocha

MODERNO

www.hotel-moderno.com
This 3-star hotel is only moments away from the Plaza Mayor and the Puerta del Sol, and has particularly welcoming staff. All 97 rooms have air-conditioning and private bathrooms.
⊞ F7 ⊠ Calle del Arenal 2 ☎ 91 531 09 00 🚇 Sol

OPERA

www.hotelopera.com
Rather plain-looking hotel but an excellent location near the opera house. All 79 rooms have satellite TV, some with balconies overlooking old Madrid.
⊞ E7 ⊠ Cuesta de Santo Domingo 2 ☎ 91 541 28 00 🚇 Ópera

SENATOR GRAN VÍA

www.hotelsenatorgranvia.com
This hotel, in the heart of the city, has an interior that neatly blends functionality and urban style. Guests can expect a CD player, iron, free minibar (nothing stronger than beer), coffee-making equipment, cable TV and bathrobes. There's also a laundry and internet access.
⊞ F7 ⊠ Gran Vía 21 ☎ 91 531 41 51 🚇 Gran Vía

TRYP ALONDRAS

www.solmelia.com
A 3-star, 72-room hotel with well-sized, air-conditioned rooms in the affluent Chamberí area. Popular with businesspeople during the week, there are attractive weekend rates for visitors. Useful for the Real Madrid stadium. Parking nearby.
⊞ F3 ⊠ José Abascal 8 ☎ 91 447 40 00 🚇 Canal, Alonso Cano, Río Rosas

ZENIT-ABEBA

www.zenithotels.com
This modern 4-star hotel is perfect for shoppers as it is just a stone's throw from Goya and Serrano streets. The décor is functional, but the rooms are spacious and comfortable. The restaurant serves traditional Spanish cuisine and opens for lunch and dinner.
⊞ K4/5 ⊠ Calle de Alcántara 63 ☎ 91 401 16 50 🚇 Diego de León

---

ROOM MATE HOTELS

HOTEL MARIO
www.room-matehoteles.com
This was the first of four jolly, budget-priced hotels in the Room Mate hotel group. Mario is well-placed, close to the Royal Palace and the Ópera. Fun designs, fun atmosphere.
⊞ E7 ⊠ Calle de Campomanes 4 ☎ 91 548 85 48 🚇 Ópera

Other Room Mate Hotels include:

HOTEL ALICIA
www.room-matehoteles.com
What was a 19th-century shoe factory is now a 34-room, designer hideaway on the corner of the Plaza Santa Ana.
⊞ F/G8 ⊠ Calle del Prado 2 ☎ 91 389 60 95 🚇 Sol, Antón Martín

HOTEL LAURA
www.room-matehoteles.com
36 stylish rooms, almost on the historic Plaza de las Descalzas, and close to the Plaza Mayor and more.
⊞ F7 ⊠ Travesía de Trujillos 3 ☎ 91 701 16 70 🚇 Callao, Santo Domingo, Ópera

HOTEL OSCAR
www.room-matehoteles.com
In buzzy Chueca, the latest Room Mate hotel opened in 2007.
⊞ G7 ⊠ Plaza Vázquez de Mella 12 ☎ 91 701 11 73 🚇 Chueca

Luxury Hotels

PRICES

Expect to pay more than €175 per night for two in a luxury room.

CASA DE MADRID
www.casademadrid.com
A short walk from the Royal Palace, this exclusive hotel is owned by art historian and interior designer, Marta Medina Muro. Each room is exquisitely decorated and furnished, some with antiques.

 E7 ✉ Calle Arrieta 2 ☎ 91 559 57 91 Ⓜ Ópera

HOSPES
www.hospes.es
A new and rather romantic boutique hotel in a classic 1883 building, this is perfectly placed within walking distance of the Prado, the Thyssen-Bornemisza, the Retiro and shopping.

✚ H7 ✉ Plaza de la Independencia 3 ☎ 91 432 29 11 Ⓜ Retiro, Banco de España

HOTEL PUERTA AMÉRICA
www.hotelpuertamerica.com
An excitingly different hotel: 19 architects/designers from 13 countries combined to create this major addition to the city's hotel scene. Expect 12 floors of vibrant colours, with a rooftop bar, black swimming pool and imaginative restaurant. Not central, but close to Serrano shopping.

✚ L3 ✉ Avenida de América 41 ☎ 91 744 54 00 Ⓜ Cartagena

HOTEL URBAN
www.derbyhotels.com
Slick and cool, the hard edges of this contemporary city centre retreat next to the Parliament building are softened by original and ancient Oriental, Latin American, African and Egyptian works of art. 96 designer bedrooms with all the latest gadgets; swimming pool. The chic Glass Bar is a popular rendezvous.

✚ G7 ✉ Carrera de San Jerónimo 34 ☎ 91 787 77 70 Ⓜ Sol, Sevilla

INTERCONTINENTAL MADRID
www.madrid.intercontinental.com
Grand and central, with lots of marble and glass, this is where business-people, politicians and film stars stay. Rooms and bathrooms are spacious and comfortable. In summer, the courtyard garden restaurant has live music. Popular brunch on Sunday. Attractive weekend rates.

✚ H4 ✉ Paseo de la Castellana 49 ☎ 91 700 73 00 Ⓜ Gregorio Marañón

ME MADRID
www.mebymelia.com
In the heart of the action, in what was once the formal old Reina Victoria (where bullfighters always stayed) is now Madrid's hip and happening hotel. Expect all the usual luxuries, from 300-thread-count linen and down pillow-top mattresses to organic, all-natural products for the shower. Stardust is provided by the Midnight Rose restaurant and its owner, Rande Gerber, husband of Cindy Crawford. 192 rooms.

✚ F8 ✉ Plaza de Santa Ana 14 ☎ 91 701 60 00 Ⓜ Anton Martín

RITZ
www.ritzmadrid.com
Spain's first luxury hotel, opened in 1910, was built for King Alfonso XIII. It lives up to its name, with 167 luxurious rooms in belle époque style. Between spring and autumn there's a delightful terrace-restaurant. Afternoon tea, taken to the sounds of a pianist, harpist or classical guitarist, is a highlight.

✚ H7 ✉ Plaza de la Lealtad 5 ☎ 91 901 67 67 Ⓜ Banco de España

HIP HOTELS

Madrid is sprouting chains of hip but affordable designer hotels. Brand names include Silken (www.hoteles-silken.com), High Tech Hoteles, under the Petit Palace label (12 hotels, mainly in Central Madrid and six more all over the city, www.hthoteles.com) and Quo (with one central hotel, www.hotelesquo.com).

Madrid is easy to get to from anywhere in the world. Although very walkable, the city also has excellent public transport. The main thing is to understand the hours when *madrileños* work, eat and play.

Planning Ahead	114–115
Getting There	116–117
Getting Around	118–119
Essential Facts	120–121
Language	122–123
Timeline	124–125

Planning Ahead

When to Go

Because of its position high on the inland plateau, Madrid can have some of the most extreme weather conditions in central Spain. Spring, early summer and autumn are the best times to visit. Although tourist crowds dwindle in winter, the weather can be bitterly cold, with temperatures rarely above freezing during the day, and icy after dark.

TIME

Spain is six hours ahead of New York, nine hours ahead of Los Angeles, and one hour ahead of the UK.

AVERAGE DAILY MAXIMUM TEMPERATURES

JAN	FEB	MAR	APR	MAY	JUN	JUL	AUG	SEP	OCT	NOV	DEC
48°F	52°F	59°F	64°F	70°F	79°F	88°F	86°F	77°F	66°F	55°F	48°F
9°C	11°C	15°C	17°C	21°C	26°C	31°C	30°C	25°C	19°C	13°C	9°C

Spring (March to mid-June) vies with autumn as the most pleasant time of year, with clear skies and sunny days, though there may be showers.
Summer (mid-June to August) is hot and dry. Rain is unusual between June and October. July and August are particularly hot.
Autumn (September to October) has little rain, sunny days and moderate temperatures.
Winter (November to February) has dry, clear days and low temperatures.

WHAT'S ON

January *Cabalgata de Reyes* (5 Jan): A procession marks the Three Wise Men's arrival. *San Antón* (17 Jan): Pets are blessed in the San Antón Church, Calle Hortaleza 63.
February *Carnival*: A week of processions and parties ends on Ash Wednesday with the ritual 'Burial of the Sardine' by the River Manzanares. *ARCO*: International contemporary arts festival.
April *Semana Santa* (Holy Week): Hooded, shoeless, chain-dragging *penitentes* bear images of Christ and the Virgin on their shoulders. On

Holy Thursday, during the procession around La Latina, the entire *barrio* takes to the streets.
May *Labour Day* and *Madrid Day* (1–2 May): Concerts region-wide; the main venue is Plaza Mayor. *San Isidro* (15 May): Nightly concerts in Plaza Mayor mark the week leading up to the saint's day of San Isidro.
June *San Antonio de la Florida* (13 Jun): Street party marks St. Antonio's feast day. *San Juan* (23 Jun): Fireworks in the Retiro to celebrate the festival of St. John.

August *Veranos de la Villa*. Madrid's summer festival of music, dance, theatre and more.
October *Festival de Otoño*: International performing arts festival (through November).
November *International Jazz Festival:* Venues all over the city.
December *Fiestas de Navidad:* Christmas lights, markets and crèches lead up to Christmas. Christmas fair in Plaza Mayor.
New Year's Eve: Thousands gather for the fireworks in the Puerta del Sol.

Madrid Online

www.spain.info
The official website for tourism in Spain, with pages in Spanish, English, German, French, Italian, Japanese and Chinese. Easy to navigate, with plenty of useful information.

www.okspain.org
Aimed at the US market, this has plenty of information, plus details of travel agents and tour operators that are Spain specialists. It also lists all the Spanish tourist offices in the USA.

www.munimadrid.es/www.esmadrid.com
The Ayuntamiento (city council) has two web-sites. The older version, ww.munimadrid.es is mainly for residents; www.esmadrid.com, with pages in English, French and other languages, is for tourists.

www.turismomadrid.es
The official site of the Comunidad de Madrid, the autonomous Region of Madrid. In Spanish and English, with pages in other languages, it also covers nearby places such as Segovia, San Lorenzo de El Escorial, Toledo and Aranjuez. Excellent.

www.eldibuk.com
Choose which part of Madrid you want to explore, click on the map and up come listings for everything from restaurants and bars to shops. Fun and funky; designed for locals as well as tourists. Spanish and English.

www.ctm-madrid.es
Come to terms with getting around Madrid by browsing the official transport site covering buses and the Metro (in English).

http://madrid.lanetro.com
Even a modicum of Spanish will be enough to access probably the best and zappiest of the Spanish-language events and listings sites, covering music, clubs, films and restaurants.

GOOD TRAVEL SITES

www.fodors.com
A complete travel-planning site. You can research prices and weather; book air tickets, cars, and rooms; ask questions (and get answers) from fellow travellers; and find links to other sites.

www.renfe.es/ingles
The official site of Spanish National Railways, with an English-language option.

www.wunderground.com
Good weather forecasting.

INTERNET ACCESS

The number of internet hotspots in Madrid is rapidly increasing. You can go online from your laptop in Barajas airport, Chamartín station, and many cafés. You can find the nearest hotspot at www.boingo.com but Wi-Fi internet access has now also become a standard service of contemporary hotels. As an alternative, there are still a very few cybercafés left where you can surf on the computers provided. The easiest to find is Café Comercial but it's a fair walk from the city hub.

Café Comercial
➕ F5 ✉ Gta de Bilbao 7
☎ 91 521 56 55
🕐 Mon–Thu 7.30–1am, Fri, Sat 8.30–2am, Sun 10–1am
Ⓜ Bilbao

Getting There

ENTRY REQUIREMENTS

● Anyone entering Spain must have a valid passport (or official identity card for EU nationals). Visa requirements are subject to change; check before making your reservations.

● As of 2007, passengers on all flights to and from Spain have to supply advance passenger information (API) to the Spanish authorities. Full names, nationality, date of birth and travel document details, namely a passport number, are required. This information is compulsory. Travel agents should be able to collect this information at the time of booking, or it can be given to staff at check-in desks.

CUSTOMS REGULATIONS

● The limits for non-EU visitors are 200 cigarettes or 50 cigars, or 250g of tobacco; 1 litre of spirits (over 22 percent) or 2 litres of fortified wine, 2 litres of still wine; 50ml of perfume. Travellers under 18 are not entitled to the tobacco and alcohol allowances.

● The guidelines for EU residents (for personal use) are 800 cigarettes, 200 cigars, 1kg tobacco; 10 litres of spirits (over 22 per cent), 20 litres of aperitifs, 90 litres of wine, of which 60 can be sparkling wine, 110 litres of beer.

AIRPORTS

All flights arrive at Madrid-Barajas Airport, 12km (7.5 miles) northeast of the city. There are four terminals: T1, T2, T3 and the newest, T4, which is used by major international airlines such as Iberia and British Airways. For more information on arrivals and departures from each terminal, go to www.aena.es ☎ 902 40 47 04.

ARRIVING BY AIR

There are tourist information areas at the airport and leaflets with information about getting to Madrid from Barajas. Terminals T1, T2 and T3 are served by Metro station Aeropuerto (Line 8); trains run from 6am to 1.30am. Terminal one is a long walk from the Metro station so allow 10 minutes to reach it. Terminal 4 is linked to the Barajas station (at the end of Line 8) by EMT bus 201, or to the Aeropuerto station with the free AENA (airport) shuttle buses that run between terminals T2, T3 and T4. A taxi from the airport to the middle of Madrid takes around 30 minutes and costs €20–€25. For more information on ground transport, www.aena.es and www.metromadrid.es.

ARRIVING BY TRAIN

RENFE (www.renfe.es), Spain's national rail company, has two mainline stations in the city. Trains from northern Europe, France and Barcelona (including the high-speed AVE train) arrive on the north side of the city at Chamartín. Trains running to and from Portugal and the south of Spain (including the high-

speed AVE train) use Atocha, close to the city centre. RENFE's UK agents are Spanish Rail (☎ 020 7725 7063, www.spanish-rail.co.uk, or the Train Line (☎ 08700 101 296). For more information, also see www.turismomadrid.es and www.esmadrid.com.

ARRIVING BY BUS

Madrid is served from other parts of Spain by many private bus companies. Inter-city coach services arrive at the Estación Sur de Autobuses on Calle Méndez Alvaro, southeast of the city centre. Buses from outside Spain (England, Portugal and France) also terminate here. For all bus information ☎ 91 468 42 00.

ARRIVING BY CAR

Drivers access Madrid via the Spanish system of toll motorways (*autopistas*) or highways (*autovías*). From France and the north, routes run along both the Mediterranean and Atlantic coasts then head towards Madrid; routes through the Pyrenees are slower but more scenic. Madrid is clearly signposted at all interchanges. From southern Spain, take the A-4 from Seville via Córdoba. From Portugal take the A-5 from Badajoz. All roads connect with the three ring roads circling Madrid: the M30, M40 and M45. Head for Paseo de la Castellana, Madrid's main artery—most central locations are easily reached from here.

SENSIBLE PRECAUTIONS

● Carry valuables in a belt, pouch or similar—not in a pocket. Be especially wary in the crowds around Plaza Mayor, Puerta del Sol and the Rastro.
● Do not keep valuables in the front section of your rucksack. If possible, wear your rucksack on your front on buses and trains.
● Be aware of street tricks around tourist attractions. These include distracting you in conversation, or spraying foam on your back and then offering to clean it off while someone else grabs your bag.

INSURANCE

Check your insurance coverage and buy a supplementary policy if necessary. EU nationals receive medical treatment with the EHIC (European Health Insurance Card), which should be obtained before travelling. Full health and travel insurance is still advised.

VISITORS WITH A DISABILITY

General access in Madrid is patchy, but gradually improving. For getting around, buses and taxis are the best bet, although only the newest buses have facilities for people with disabilities. New buildings and museums have excellent wheelchair access, older attractions have yet to be converted, and churches are particularly difficult. English-language advice is available on www.access-able.com. FAMMA is the Spanish association that deals with all disabilities (in Spanish only, www.famma.org).

Getting Around

BUSES

● The bus system is efficient and far-reaching, with regular scheduled services to all parts of the city and its suburbs.

● Finding your way is made easy, as the various routes and stops are shown at every bus stop on a plan.

● There are two types of buses—the standard red bus and the yellow microbus. Both operate between 6am and midnight, and charge €1 for each one-way ride in the city, though the *bono* or Metrobus ticket giving 10 rides costs €7 (see below).

● Night buses (known locally as *buhos*, meaning owls) operate from Plaza de Cibeles to many suburbs between midnight and 6am and the tickets cost the same as during the day. The night bus service is not as punctual as the day-time one.

● Bus information offices are located in Plaza de Cibeles and Puerta del Sol, where you can pick up route maps and schedules.

● For full bus information see www.emtmadrid.es

METRO

● The Metro system is very reliable and the best way of getting around the city quickly.

● There are 12 lines, each with a different colour and number shown on route maps and at stations.

● The Metro is constantly expanding and improving. Most of the new stations are on the outskirts of this fast-growing city, built to speed commuters to and from work. Most of all, the Metro is clean and safe for visitors.

● The system is split into zones, with most of it in Zone A, while the outlying areas and lines are in zones B1, B2 and B3.

● The two airport terminals are classed as a separate zone, for which a supplementary fee is charged.

● A single journey ticket (*sencilla*) within Zone A costs €1 (€1.90 for all zones), but you can get a Metrobus ticket, giving 10 rides, for €7.

● A tourist card (*abono turistico*) is also

available for visitors, and can be for 1, 2, 3, 5 or 7 days. A 1-day pass costs €5 for Zone A, a 7-day pass €22.60, with reductions of up to 50 per cent for children. You would need to make six Metro or bus trips a day for it to work out cheaper than a Metrobus ticket.

● You can buy tickets (also valid for the buses) from Metro stations in the city and from some newsagents and tobacconists.

● The Metro system runs from 6am to 2am; schedule information and a full Metro map are available from www.metromadrid.es (☎ 902 44 44 03), or from any station. Also see www.ctm-madrid.es, which has all the information in English as well as Spanish.

● Metro trains run about every 3 to 6 minutes from Monday to Friday; this extends to every 15 minutes after midnight, and there are slightly fewer trains on weekends.

● It's best to avoid the rush hours, generally 7–9.30am and 7–9pm, when it gets very busy.

TAXIS

● Official taxis are white with a diagonal red stripe. A green light on the roof shows when they are free.

● The standard base taxi fare is €2.05, with a charge of €0.98 for every further kilometre. There is a supplement payable on Sundays and holidays, and for certain destinations, such as the rail station, airport and bullring.

● Make sure the meter is turned on and set at the base fare for your journey.

● The major private taxi companies in Madrid are TeleTaxi (☎ 91 371 21 31) and Radio Taxi (☎ 91 447 32 32). You can book your taxi online at www.radiotaxigremial.com

TRAINS

● Chamartín, north of Plaza de Castilla, is the terminus for northern destinations. It is linked by a through line with Atocha.

● *Cercanías* refers to local and suburban trains, *largo recorrido* to intercity and long-distance trains.

GUIDED WALKS

Official guided tours of the city leave regularly from the Madrid Tourism Centre on Plaza Mayor 27. They go on foot, by bus and even by bicycle. There are 28 different themes, such as the Oldest Madrid, Madrid in Films, Great Writers and 20th-century Architecture. For dates and times visit www.esmadrid.com. It is important to book ahead at the tourist office or by phoning ☎ 91 588 29 06. Cost is €3.30 per person.

For a really special experience, get under the skin of Madrid on a tour run by the Spanish-American husband and wife team of Carlos and Jennifer Galvin, who run LeTango Tours. They take you to the places that locals go, explaining how various traditions began and why they persist. One of the most entertaining walks is a foodie-oriented 'tapas tour' (☎ 91 369 47 52, mobile 661 752 458, toll free US 1 866 866 5107; www.letango.com).

A British guide with a passion for the Duke of Wellington, Stephen Drake-Jones also runs the Wellington Society, devoted to understanding the history of Spain in general and Madrid in particular (mobile 609 143 203; www.wellsoc.org).

Essential Facts

LOST AND FOUND

● Municipal Lost Property Office (Oficina de Objetos Perdidos) ⊠ Paseo del Molino 7 ☎ 91 527 95 90 🇶 Legazpi ● Mon–Fri 9–2
● For objects lost on a bus: EMT ⊠ Cerro de la Plata 4 ☎ 902 50 78 50 🇶 Pacífico ● Mon–Fri 9–2. Ask for *objetos perdidos*.
● To claim insurance, you must obtain a *denuncia* (signed statement of loss) from a police station.

MONEY

The euro (€) is the official currency of Spain. Banknotes are in denominations of 5, 10, 20, 50, 100, 200 and 500 euros, and coins in denominations of 1, 2, 5, 10, 20, 50 cents and 1 and 2 euros.

10 euros

50 euros

200 euros

500 euros

ELECTRICITY

● The standard current is 220 volts.
● Plugs are of the round two-pin type.

ETIQUETTE

● Spaniards rarely form orderly queues, but are generally aware of their place in the service order.
● There are clearly marked 'No Smoking' areas in many restaurants. Smoking on buses and trains is banned.
● It is considered good manners to issue a general hello (*buenos días* in the morning; *buenas tardes* in the afternoon/evening) when entering a shop, office, etc. and to say goodbye (*adios*) when leaving.
● Do not be worried about using your voice to attract attention in bars and restaurants. Say *Oiga* (Oy-ga, literally 'hear me'), and add *por favor* (thank you).
● Drinks are normally paid for before you leave the bar, not on a round-by-round basis.
● Tipping is discretionary, but 5 per cent is normal practice.

MONEY MATTERS

● Most major travellers' cheques can be changed at banks. American Express offers the best travellers' cheque rates.
● Credit cards are now accepted in all large establishments and many smaller ones.
● There are many multilingual ATM/cash machines.

OPENING HOURS

● Shops: 9–1.30, 5–8; department stores: 9–9. Some are open Sundays.
● Churches: 9.30–1.30, 5–7.30. Many only open half an hour before a service.
● Museums: many close on Mondays.
● Banks: Mon–Fri 9–2; between October and May many banks open from 9–1 on Saturdays.

MAIL

● Buy stamps (*sellos*) from a post office

(*oficina de Correos*) or tobacconists (*estancos*), indicated by a yellow and brown sign.

● Madrid's most central post office is ✉ Plaza de Cibeles ☎ 91 523 06 94 (for general postal enquiries 902 19 71 97) 🕐 Mon–Fri 8.30am–9.30pm, Sat 8.30–2. The post office at Mariano Fernández 1 is open six days a week: weekdays 8.30am–10pm, Sat 9.30am–10pm (☎ 91 459 50 29).

● Post boxes are mostly yellow with two slots, one marked 'Madrid' and the other for everywhere else (*Provincias y extranjero*).

TELEPHONES

● Public telephones take €1 and €2 coins and 2c, 5c, 10c, 20c and 50c coins.

● Phone cards are available from newsstands; some phones accept credit cards.

● The technology for mobile, or cell, phones in Spain is GSM, which may be incompatible with some countries, for example, the USA or Japan. Tri-band mobiles/cell phones will work. Check to make sure your phone will work and what the cost of calls will be. Charges for roaming—using your phone in another country—can be high.

● To call Spain from the UK dial 00 34 followed by 91 for Madrid and then the seven digit number. To call the UK from Spain dial 00 44 and omit the zero from the area code. To call Australia dial 00 61.

● To call Spain from the US dial 011 34 followed by 91 for Madrid and then the seven digit number. To call the US from Spain dial 001.

MEDICINES AND HEALTHCARE

● Pharmacies (*farmacias*) are indicated by a flashing green cross; they are usually open 9.30–2 and 5–8. All post a list of *farmacias de guardia* (all-night chemists) and highlight the closest ones.

● Spanish pharmacists are qualified to give over-the-counter advice on healthcare and many minor ailments, but for serious conditions you should ask for directions to the nearest hospital or doctor's office.

EMERGENCY NUMBERS

● Police (Local) ☎ 092
● Police (National) ☎ 091
● Police (Guardia Civil) ☎ 062
● Police, Ambulance, Fire ☎ 112
● Fire station: Madrid ☎ 080
● SATE is a special 24-hour service for foreign tourists who need to report crimes to the police. In Spanish, English and French ☎ 90 210 21 12; www.es.madrid.com.

TOILETS

Gone are the days when tourists needed to worry about hygiene in toilets in restaurants and bars. Modern Spain has modern toilet facilities.

TOURIST OFFICES

Plaza Mayor 27 ☎ 91 588 16 36 🕐 Daily 9.30–8.30
Calle del Duque de Medinaceli 2 ☎ 91 429 49 51 🕐 Mon–Sat, 9.30–8.30, Sun, hols 9.30–2
Estación de Atocha ☎ 91 528 46 30 🕐 Mon–Sat 9.30–8.30, Sun, hols 9.30–2
Estación de Chamartín ☎ 91 315 99 76 🕐 Mon–Sat 9.30–8.30, Sun, hols 9.30–2
Madrid-Barajas Airport Terminal 1 ☎ 91 305 86 56 🕐 Daily 9.30–8.30
Terminal 4 ☎ 902 10 00 07 🕐 Daily 9.30–8.30

Language

English is now the second language of many, if not most, Europeans. Staff in Madrid's hotels, many restaurants and even many shops speak English. However, it is fun to try a few words in Spanish and, of course, any efforts are appreciated! In bars, the tapas on offer are often chalked up on a board; perfect for trying out your Spanish.

PRONUNCIATION

c before an *e* or an *i*, and *z* are like *th* in thin
c in other cases is like *c* in cat
g before an *e* or an *i*, and *j* are a guttural sound which does not exist in English—rather like the *ch* in loch
g in other cases is like *g* in get
h is normally silent
ll is similar to y
y is like the *i* in onion
Use the formal *usted* when speaking to strangers; the informal *tu* for friends or younger people.

COURTESIES	
good morning	*buenos días*
good afternoon/evening	*buenas tardes*
good night	*buenas noches*
hello (informal)	*hola*
goodbye (informal)	*hasta luego/hasta pronto*
hello (answering the phone)	*¿Diga?*
goodbye	*adios*
please	*por favor*
thank you	*gracias*
you're welcome	*de nada*
how are you? (formal)	*¿Como está?*
how are you? (informal)	*¿Que tal?*
I'm fine	*estoy bien*
I'm sorry	*lo siento*
excuse me (in a bar)	*oiga*
excuse me (in a crowd)	*perdón*

USEFUL WORDS	
I don't know	*No lo sé*
I don't think so	*Creo que no*
I think so	*Creo que sí*
It doesn't matter	*No importa*
Where?	*¿Dónde?*
When?	*¿Cuándo?*
Why?	*¿Por qué?*
What?	*¿Qué?*
Who?	*¿Quién?*
How?	*¿Cómo?*
How much/ many?	*¿Cuánto / cuántos?*
Is/are there?	*¿Hay?*
ticket	*entrada*

BASIC VOCABULARY

yes/no	sí/no
I do not understand	no entiendo
left/right	izquierda/derecha
entrance/exit	entrada/salida
open/closed	abierto/cerrado
good/bad	bueno/malo
big/small	grande/pequeño
with/without	con/sin
more/less	más/menos
hot/cold	caliente/frío
early/late	temprano/tarde
here/there	aquí/allí
today/tomorrow	hoy/mañana
yesterday	ayer
how much is it?	¿cuánto es?
where is the...?	¿dónde está...?
do you have...?	¿tiene...?
I'd like.....	me gustaría...
I don't speak Spanish	no hablo español

FOOD

apple	manzana
banana	plátano
beans	habichuelas
chicken	pollo
clams	almejas
duck	pato
fish/seafood	pescado/marisco
fruit	fruta
lamb	cordero
lettuce	lechuga
lobster	langosta
meat	carne
melon	melón
orange	naranja
pork	cerdo
shrimp	gambas
squid	calamares
tomato	tomate
tuna	atún
turkey	pavo

IN THE RESTAURANT

smoking allowed	se permite fumar
no smoking	se prohibe fumar
menu	la carta
fork	tenedor
knife	cuchillo
spoon	cuchara
napkin	servilleta
glass of wine	copa
glass of beer	caña
water (mineral)	agua (mineral)
still	sin gas
sparkling/bubbles	con gas
coffee (with milk)	café (con leche)
May I have the bill/check	¿La cuenta, por favor?
Do you take credit cards?	¿Aceptan tarjetas de crédito?
tavern	mesón/taberna
cakes	pasteles
small snacks	pinchos
sandwiches	bocadillos
set dishes	platos combinados

SHOPPING

ATM/cash machine	Cajero
I want to buy...	Quiero comprar...
belt	cinturón
blouse	blusa
dress	vestido
shirt	camisa
shoes	zapatas
skirt	falda
tie	corbata
small	pequeño
medium	mediano
large	grande
cotton	algodón
silk	seda
wool	lana
café	cafetería
breakfast	desayuno
lunch	almuerzo
dinner	cena

Timeline

BEFORE AD800

Iberian tribes inhabited Madrid from around 1000BC. The Romans ruled the Iberian peninsula between 218BC and the 5th century AD and Madrid became a stopping place.

In AD711, Muslims defeated the Visigoths—areas of Spain came under Muslim rule for 800 years.

854 Muhammad I of Córdoba founds the city of Madrid.

1083 Madrid is recaptured by Alfonso VI; Christians, Jews and Muslims all inhabit the city.

1202 Alfonso VIII recognizes Madrid as a city by giving it Royal Statutes.

1309 The Cortes, or Parliament, meets in Madrid for the first time.

1469 The marriage of Catholic monarchs Ferdinand and Isabella unites Aragon and Castile.

1492 The conquest of Granada completes the unification of Spain. Spain begins a 200-year period of imperial power, and expels the Jews.

1561 Philip II establishes Court in Madrid: a cultural 'Golden Age' begins.

1578 Philip III (1598–1621) is the first monarch to be born in Madrid.

1617–19 Plaza Mayor is built.

1759 Charles III begins a modernization schedule for Madrid.

1808–12 French occupation; famine kills 30,000. Spanish rule restored 1814.

Below, from left to right: The interview of Columbus with Queen Isabella; Ferdinand the Catholic; Philip II; statue of Philip III in the Plaza Mayor; General Francisco Franco; statue of the painter Goya

1819 Prado museum opens.

1851 The Madrid–Aranjuez railway line is inaugurated.

1873 The First Republic is declared.

1917 Spain faces a general strike.

1919 The first Metro line in Madrid opens.

1931 The Second Republic is declared.

1936–39 The Spanish Civil War takes place, sparked by uprising in North Africa. The Nationalists win, and the long dictatorship of General Franco follows.

1975 General Franco dies; King Juan Carlos is declared his successor.

1977 The first democratic general election.

1986 Spain joins the EEC (now EU).

1992 Madrid is European City of Culture.

2002 Spain adopts the euro: a landmark in the move to mainstream Europe.

2007 Madrid's Metro system becomes the world's third largest .

2010 Madrid hosts the final of football's UEFA Champions League in May.

MADRID PEOPLE

Charles III
Charles III is often known as 'the best mayor that Madrid ever had'. More than any other single historical figure, he is responsible for today's Madrid. He came to the throne in 1759 and was a keen proponent of Enlightenment ideals.

Cervantes
Cervantes is the author of *Don Quixote*, believed by some to be the first novel ever written. A tax collector, he wrote *Don Quixote* while in jail for manipulating accounts. He died in Madrid in 1616.

Goya
Goya (1746–1828) is the painter most readily associated with Madrid, though he neither was born nor died here. He settled in Madrid in 1774 and became Court painter to Charles IV in 1789.

GOYA

Index

A
accommodation 107–112
air travel 116–117
America Museum 9, 30
antiques 12, 61, 62, 78
Aquópolis 101
Arab Wall 37
Aranjuez 106
Arco de los Cuchilleros 51
ATMs 120
Ayuntamiento 59

B
banks 120
Basilica de San Francisco El Grande 36
Botanical Garden 77
Botero statues 88
budget travellers 17, 109
bullfighting 98
buses
  city buses 118
  long-distance 117

C
cabaret 63
cable car 24, 34
CaixaForum 56
La Calcografía Nacional 55
Calderón de la Barca, Pedro 56
Calle Mayor 56
Calle del Mesón de Paredes 56
Calle de Preciados 10
Los Caprichos de Alameda de Osuna 101
Casa de Campo 8, 24
Casa de Cisneros 59
Casa Museo Lope de Vega 56–57
Casa de las Siete Chimeneas 88
Casa de la Villa 59
Casón del Buen Retiro 76
Catedral de la Almudena 8, 25
Centro 43–66
  entertainment and nightlife 63–64
  map 44–45
  restaurants 65–66
  shopping 61–62
  sights 46–59
  walk 60
Centro Cultural Conde Duque 36
Cerralbo Museum 9, 28–29

Cervantes 37, 125
children's entertainment 17
Chueca and the north 81–94
  entertainment and nightlife 93
  map 82–83
  restaurants 94
  shopping 92
  sights 84–90
  walk 91
chupito 93
cinemas 40
City, Museum of the 88–89
climate and seasons 114
clubs 18, 40, 63, 64, 79, 93
Colegiata de San Isidro 57
Costume, Museum of 9, 31
Congreso de los Diputados 58
credit cards 120
crime 117
Cuatro Torres Business Area 101
customs regulations 116
cybercafés 115

D
Debod Temple 34
disabilities, visitors with 108, 117
driving 117

E
eating out 14–15, 120
  Madrid cuisine 15, 66
  meal times 14
  regional cuisine 15, 41, 42
  tapas 14, 15, 17, 80
  see *also* restaurants
Edificio España 37
electricity 120
emergency telephone numbers 121
Engraving Plates Museum 55
entertainment and nightlife 13
  Centro 63–64
  Chueca and the north 93
  Jerónimos and the east 79
  Palacio and the west 40
Ermita de San Antonio de la Florida 8, 26

El Escorial 103
Estación de Atocha 76
Estación de Príncipe Pío 36–37
El Estadio Santiago Bernabéu 100
etiquette 120
excursions 103–106

F
fans 61
fashion shopping 10–11, 12, 39, 62, 92
Faunia 101
festivals and events 114
flamenco 61–62, 63, 64
food shopping 11, 12, 61–62, 92
Fundación Juan March 88

G
gifts and souvenirs 11
Glass Palace 73
Goya 26, 36, 52, 54–55, 71, 77, 88, 125
Gran Vía 57–58
Guernica (Picasso) 47
guitars 62, 92

H
history 124–125
hostales 108, 109
hotels 18, 108, 109–112

I
Iglesia de San Antón 88
insurance 117

J
Jardines del Descubrimiento 76
Jardines de las Vistillas 37
Jerónimos and the east 67–80
  entertainment and nightlife 79
  map 68–69
  restaurants 79–80
  shopping 78
  sights 70–77

K
Kilometre Zero 52

L
language 122–123
Lasso de Castilla 58–59
leather goods 11, 39, 92

Lope de Vega, Felix 56, 57
lost property 120

M
Madrid environs 95–106
  excursions 103–106
  map 96–97
  sights 98–102
Madrid Stock Exchange
  77
mail services 120–121
markets 11, 53, 62
medicines 121
Metro 118–119
Monasterio de las
  Descalzas Reales 9, 50
Monasterio de la
  Encarnación 9, 27
money 120
Muralla Árabe 37
Museo de América 9, 30
Museo Arqueológico
  Nacional 76
Museo Cerralbo 9, 28–29
Museo de la Ciudad
  88–89
Museo de Escultura al Aire
  Libre 89
Museo Lázaro Galdiano 9,
  84–85
Museo Nacional Reina
  Sofía 9, 46–47
Museo del Prado 9, 70–71
Museo Romántico 89
Museo Sorolla 9, 86–87
Museo Taurino 98
Museo Thyssen-
  Bornemisza 9, 48–49
Museo del Traje 9, 31

N
nightlife 13, 18, 40, 63–64,
  79, 93

O
opening hours 120
opera 40

P
Palacio de Cristál 73
Palacio de Linares 74
Palacio Real 9, 32–33
Palacio Real de El Pardo
  102
Palacio and the west
  20–42
  entertainment and
    nightlife 40

map 22–23
  restaurants 41–42
  shopping 39
  sights 24–37
  walk 38
El Pardo 102
Parque de Atracciones 24
Parque Florido 85
Parque del Oeste 9, 34
Parque del Retiro 9, 13,
  72–73
Paseo de la Castellana 89
passports and visas 116
pensiones 108
personal safety 117
pharmacies 121
Plaza de la Cibeles 8, 74
Plaza del Conde de
  Barajas 58
Plaza de las Cortes 58
Plaza de Dos de Mayo
  90
Plaza de España 37
Plaza de la Lealtad 76–77
Plaza Mayor 8, 13, 51
Plaza de Oriente 8, 35
Plaza de la Paja 58–59
Plaza de Santa Ana 59
Plaza de Toros 8, 98–99
Plaza de la Villa 59
police 121
post offices 121
Prado 9, 70–71
public transport 118–119
Puerta de Alcalá 8, 75
Puerta de Europa 102
Puerta del Sol 8, 38, 52,
  60, 91

R
El Rastro 8, 53
Real Academia de Bellas
  Artes 8, 54–55
Real Fábrica de Tapices 77
Real Jardín Botánico 77
Real Madrid 4, 8, 100
restaurants 15, 18
  Centro 65–66
  Chueca and the north
    94
  Jerónimos and the east
    79–80
  Palacio and the west
    41–42
Retiro Park 9, 13, 72–73
Royal Academy of Fine
  Arts 8, 54–55
Royal Palace 9, 32–33

Royal Shoeless Nuns'
  Convent 9, 50
Royal Tapestry Factory 77
Royal Theatre 35, 40

S
Sala del Canal de Isabel II
  90
sales tax 11
San Jerónimo El Real 77
San Nicolás de los Servitas
  37
San Pedro El Viejo 59
Santa Bárbara (Las Salesas
  Reales) 90
Segovia 103
shopping 10–12, 16
  see also each chapter
smoking etiquette 120
Sorolla Museum 9, 86–87
stamps and coins market
  62

T
tapas 14, 15, 17, 80
taxis 119
Teatro Real 35, 40
teleférico 24, 34
telephones 121
Templo de Debod 34
theme parks 101, 102
Thyssen-Bornemisza
  Museum 9, 48–49
time differences 114
tipping 14, 120
toilets 121
Toledo 104–105
Torre de los Lujanes 59
Torre Madrid 37
Torres Kio 102
tourist information 115, 121
train services 116, 119
travellers' cheques 120
two-day itinerary 6–7

W
walks
  east from Sol 60
  north from Sol 91
  west from Sol 38
walks, guided 119
Warner Bros Park 102
water parks 101
websites 115

Z
zarzuela 64
Zoo-Aquarium de Madrid 24

CITYPACK TOP 25
Madrid

WRITTEN BY Jonathan Holland
ADDITIONAL WRITING Paul Wade and Kathy Arnold
UPDATED BY Nicholas Inman and Clara Villanueva
COVER DESIGN AND DESIGN WORK Jacqueline Bailey
INDEXER Marie Lorimer
IMAGE RETOUCHING AND REPRO Sarah Montgomery and James Tims
EDITORIAL MANAGEMENT Apostrophe S Limited
SERIES EDITOR Marie-Claire Jefferies

© **AA MEDIA LIMITED 2010**

First published 1997
New edition 2008
Information verified and updated for 2010

Colour separation by Keenes, Andover, UK
Printed and bound by Leo Paper Products, China

A CIP catalogue record for this book is available from the British Library.

ISBN 978-0-7495-5493-4

Published by AA Publishing, a trading name of AA Media Limited, whose registered office is Fanum House, Basing View, Basingstoke, Hampshire RG21 4EA. Registered number 06112600.

A04019
Maps in this title produced from mapping © MAIRDUMONT / Falk Verlag 2010
Transport map © Communicarta Ltd, UK

The Automobile Association wishes to thank the following photographers, companies and picture libraries for their assistance in the preparation of this book.

Abbreviations for the picture credits are as follows – (t) top; (b) bottom; (l) left; (r) right; (c) centre; (AA) AA World Travel Library.

Front cover AA/M Jourdan; **back cover (i)** AA/M Jourdan; **(ii)** AA/C Sawyer; **(iii)** AA/M Chaplow; **(iv)** AA/M Jourdan; **1** AA/R Strange; **2** AA/M Jourdan; **3** AA/M Jourdan; **4t** AA/M Jourdan; **4c** AA/M Jourdan; **5t** AA/M Jourdan; **5c** AA/M Jourdan; **6t** AA/M Jourdan; **6cl** AA/R Strange; **6cr** AA/M Chaplow; **6bl** AA/M Chaplow; **6bc** AA/M Jourdan; **6br** AA/S Day; **7t** AA/M Jourdan; **7cl** AA/M Jourdan; **7cr** AA/C Sawyer; **7bl** AA/M Chaplow; **7br** AA/M Jourdan; **8** AA/M Jourdan; **9** AA/M Jourdan; **10t** AA/M Jourdan; **10ct** AA/M Jourdan; **10c** AAM Chaplow; **10cb** AA/M Jourdan; **10/11** AA/M Jourdan; **11t** AA/M Jourdan; **11ct** AA/M Jourdan; **11c** AA/R Strange; **11cb** AA/M Chaplow; **12t** AA/M Jourdan; **12b** AA/R Strange; **13t** AA/M Jourdan; **13ct** AA/M Jourdan; **13c** AA/M Jourdan; **13cb** AA/M Jourdan; **13b** AA/M Jourdan; **14t** AA/M Jourdan; **14cr** AA/M Jourdan; **14c** AA/M Chaplow; **14cb** AA/M Jourdan; **14b** AA/M Chaplow; **15t** AA/M Jourdan; **15b** AA/M Chaplow; **16t** AA/M Jourdan; **16ct** AA/M Chaplow; **16c** AA/M Jourdan; **16cb** AA/M Chaplow; **16b** AA/J Edmanson; **17t** AA/M Jourdan; **17ct** AA/M Jourdan; **17c** AA/M Chaplow; **17cb** AA/M Chaplow; **17b** AA/J A Tims; **18t** AA/M Jourdan; **18ct** AA/M Chaplow; **18c** AA/C Sawyer; **18cb** Photodisc; **18b** Brand X Pictures; **19(i)** AA/M Jourdan; **19(ii)** AA/M Jourdan; **19(iii)** AA/M Jourdan; **19(iv)** AA/R Strange; **19(v)** AA/M Chaplow; **20/21** AA/M Jourdan; **24l** AA/M Chaplow; **24r** AA/M Chaplow; **25l** AA/R Strange; **25c** AA/R Strange; **25r** AA/M Jourdan; **26l** AA/M Chaplow; **26r** AA/R Strange; **27l** AA/M Chaplow; **27r** AA/P Enticknap; **28** Museo Cerralbo; **28/29** Museo Cerralbo; **30l** AA/R Strange; **30r** AA/R Strange; **31l** Museo Traje; **31r** Museo Traje; **32** AA/M Jourdan; **32/33t** AA/M Jourdan; **32/33b** AA/M Jourdan; **33t** AA/M Chaplow; **33cl** AA/M Jourdan; **33cr** AA/M Jourdan; **34l** AA/R Strange; **34r** AA/R Strange; **35l** AA/M Chaplow; **35c** AA/M Chaplow; **35r** AA/M Chaplow; **36t** AA/M Jourdan; **36b** AA/M Jourdan; **37t** AA/M Jourdan; **37b** AA/M Jourdan; **38** AA/M Jourdan; **39** AA/R Strange; **40** AA/M Jourdan; **41** Imagestate; **42** Imagestate; **43** AA/R Strange; **46** AA/M Jourdan; **47l** AA/M Jourdan; **47c** AA/M Chaplow; **47r** AA/M Jourdan; **48** AA/M Chaplow; **48/49** AA/M Jourdan; **50l** AA/R Strange; **50r** AA/M Chaplow; **51l** AA/M Jourdan; **51c** AA/M Jourdan; **51r** AA/M Chaplow; **51l** AA/M Jourdan; **52c** AA/M Chaplow; **52r** AA/M Chaplow; **53l** AA/M Jourdan; **53r** AA/M Jourdan; **54l** The Vision of St. Alphonsus Rodriguez (1533–1617), Zurbarán, Francisco de (1598–1664), Real Academia de Bellas Artes de San Fernando, Madrid, Spain, Bridgeman Art Library; **54/55** Alamy (Alex Segre); **56t** AA/M Jourdan; **56b** AA/M Jourdan; **57t** AA/M Jourdan; **57bl** AA/M Chaplow; **57br** AA/M Chaplow; **58t** AA/M Jourdan; **58bl** AA/M Chaplow; **58br** AA/M Chaplow; **59t** AA/M Jourdan; **59bl** AA/J Edmanson; **59br** AA/M Jourdan; **60** AA/M Jourdan; **61** AA/R Strange; **62** AA/R Strange; **63** AA/M Jourdan; **64** AA/M Jourdan; **65** Imagestate; **66** Imagestate; **67** AA/J Edmanson; **70l** AA/M Jourdan; **70/71t** AA/M Jourdan; **70c** AA/M Jourdan; **70/71c** AA/M Jourdan; **71t** AA/M Jourdan; **71cl** AA/M Jourdan; **71cr** AA/M Jourdan; **72** AA/M Jourdan; **73l** AA/M Chaplow; **73r** AA/M Chaplow; **73r** AA/M Chaplow; **74l** AA/M Jourdan; **74r** AA/M Jourdan; **75l** AA/R Strange; **75r** AA/J Edmanson; **76t** AA/M Jourdan; **76bl** AA/M Chaplow; **76br** AA/M Chaplow; **77t** AA/M Jourdan; **77b** AA/M Chaplow; **78** AA/R Strange; **79t** AA/M Jourdan; **79c** Imagestate; **80** Imagestate; **81** AA/R Strange; **84** Alamy (INTERFOTO Pressebildagentur); **84/85** The Crusaders before Jerusalem (oil on canvas), Velázquez, Eugenio Lucas (1817–70), Museo Lazaro Galdiano, Madrid, Spain, Bridgeman Art Library; **86** AA/M Chaplow; **86/87** AA/R Strange; **88t** AA/M Jourdan; **88c** Museo de la Cuidad; **89t** AA/M Jourdan; **89b** AA/M Chaplow; **90t** AA/M Jourdan; **90b** AA/R Strange; **91** AA/M Jourdan; **92** AA/R Strange; **93** AA/M Jourdan; **94** Imagestate; **95** AA/M Jourdan; **98l** AA/M Jourdan; **98r** AA/M Jourdan; **99** AA/M Jourdan; **100l** AA/M Chaplow; **100r** AA/M Chaplow; **101t** AA/M Jourdan; **101** AA/C Sawyer; **102t** AA/M Jourdan; **102b** Alamy (Kevin Foy); **103t** AA/M Chaplow; **103lbl** AA/M Chaplow; **103bl** AA/M Chaplow; **103br** AA/M Chaplow; **103rbr** AA/M Chaplow; **104** AA/M Chaplow; **105t** AA/M Chaplow; **105bl** AA/M Chaplow; **105bc** AA/M Chaplow; **105br** AA/M Chaplow; **106t** AA/M Chaplow; **106bl** AA/J Edmanson; **106bc** AA/J Edmanson; **106br** AA/J Edmanson; **107** AA/C Sawyer; **108t** AA/C Sawyer; **108ct** Photodisc; **108c** Photodisc; **108cb** Photodisc; **108b** Stockbyte; **109** AA/C Sawyer; **110** AA/C Sawyer; **111** AA/C Sawyer; **112** AA/C Sawyer; **113** AA/M Chaplow; **114** AA/M Chaplow; **115** AA/M Chaplow; **116** AA/M Chaplow; **117t** AA/M Chaplow; **117b** AA/M Chaplow; **118t** AA/M Chaplow; **118b** AA/R Strange; **119** AA/M Chaplow; **120** AA/M Chaplow; **120bl** European Central Bank; **121** AA/M Chaplow; **122t** AA/M Jourdan; **122b** AA/M Chaplow; **124t** AA/M Chaplow; **124bl** AA; **124bc** AA; **124br** AA; **125t** AA/M Chaplow; **125bl** AA/M Jourdan; **125bc** Illustrated London News; **125r** AA/M Jourdan

Every effort has been made to trace the copyright holders, and we apologise in advance for any unintentional omissions or errors. We would be pleased to apply any corrections in any following edition of this publication.

CITYPACK TOP 25
Madrid

JONATHAN HOLLAND
ADDITIONAL WRITING BY PAUL WADE AND KATHY ARNOLD

AA Publishing
If you have any comments or suggestions for this guide you can contact the editor at
Citypack@theAA.com

How to Use This Book

KEY TO SYMBOLS

✚ Map reference to the accompanying fold-out map

✉ Address

☎ Telephone number

🕐 Opening/closing times

🍴 Restaurant or café

🚆 Nearest rail station

Ⓜ Nearest subway (Metro) station

🚌 Nearest bus route

⛴ Nearest riverboat or ferry stop

♿ Facilities for visitors with disabilities

❓ Other practical information

▷ Further information

ℹ Tourist information

✋ Admission charges: Expensive (over €6), Moderate (€3–€6), and Inexpensive (€3 or less)

★ Major Sight   ★ Minor Sight

👣 Walks   🚐 Excursions

🏬 Shops

🎵 Entertainment and Nightlife

🍴 Restaurants

This guide is divided into four sections

• **Essential Madrid:** An introduction to the city and tips on making the most of your stay.
• **Madrid by Area:** We've broken the city into five areas, and recommended the best sights, shops, entertainment venues, nightlife and restaurants in each one. Suggested walks help you to explore on foot.
• **Where to Stay:** The best hotels, whether you're looking for luxury, budget or something in between.
• **Need to Know:** The info you need to make your trip run smoothly, including getting about by public transport, weather tips, emergency phone numbers and useful websites.

Navigation In the Madrid by Area chapter, we've given each area its own colour, which is also used on the locator maps throughout the book and the map on the inside front cover.

Maps The fold-out map accompanying this book is a comprehensive street plan of Madrid. The grid on this fold-out map is the same as the grid on the locator maps within the book. We've given grid references within the book for each sight and listing.